CONTENTS

THE LAB MANUAL
to accompany

Henry

THE
EFFECTIVE
READER
Third Edition

Mary Dubbé
Thomas Nelson Community College

Longman

Boston Columbus Indianapolis New York San Francisco Upper Saddle River

Amsterdam Cape Town Dubai London Madrid Milan Munich Paris Montreal Toronto

Delhi Mexico City São Paulo Sydney Hong Kong Seoul Singapore Taipei Tokyo

The Lab Manual to accompany Henry, *The Effective Reader, Third Edition*

3 4 5 6 7 8 9 10–CW–13 12 11

Longman is an
imprint of

www.pearsonhighered.com

ISBN 10: 0-205-82827-2
ISBN 13: 978-0-205-82827-2

For Students:

This Lab Manual is a collection of 78 activities designed to provide additional practice and enrichment for the skills in *The Effective Reader*. Each chapter consists of six lab activities that will provide you with additional practice and assessment of your skills.

You will practice applying the strategies you are learning to numerous textbook paragraphs and longer passages from a wide range of academic disciplines. You will continue to learn new vocabulary in many activities, practice identifying main ideas and supporting details, use outlines and concept maps to make sure you understand the reading selections, and practice your inference skills in the contexts of excerpts taken primarily from current college textbooks.

This lab manual also includes a skills awareness inventory sheet for each of the tutorial tests that you may take before you begin the course as well as achievement tests to discover how much you have learned by the end of the course. Three pairs of tests are available: one is specifically designed for students in Florida who must pass the Florida State Basic Skills Exit Test, a second is for Texas students who need to take the THEA, and a third is intended for more general use. (Your instructor will provide the most appropriate one for you.) Answer sheets are available in the back of the Lab Manual as well as report forms that foster metacognition. These report forms can be used as a portfolio activity to help you assess your learning and growth.

Finally, at the end of the manual is a report form where you can record your grades and keep track of your progress. Mastering these skills will ensure that you are effectively prepared for your academic subjects.

For Instructors:

The Lab Manual is a collection of 78 activities designed to provide additional practice and enrichment for the skills in *The Effective Reader*. Each chapter consists of six lab activities that can be used to add flexibility and interest to the classroom or for additional practice and for assessment purposes.

These lab activities provide students with a range of opportunities to practice becoming effective readers. The chapters of *The Effective Reader* include numerous practices, applications, review tests, and mastery tests. The Lab Manual offers two practice exercises, two review tests and two mastery tests that mirror the design of the text and emphasize the reading skills and applications students need to succeed in college. Students apply the strategies they are learning to numerous textbook paragraphs and longer passages from a wide range of academic disciplines.

Each activity in the Lab Manual is carefully constructed to ensure that students understand the purpose of the activity and can complete it successfully. The practice exercises begin with a succinct statement of the objective. The Answer Key to the Lab Manual can be found online at www.ablongman.com/henry and by choosing *The Effective Reader*. A report form is available at the end of the manual for students to keep a record of their scores and to track their progress.

The lab manual also includes a skills awareness inventory sheet for each of the tutorial tests that students may take before they begin the course as well as achievement tests to discover how much they have learned by the end of the course. Three pairs of tests are available for students using *The Effective Reader*: one is specifically designed for students in Florida who must pass the Florida State Basic Skills Exit Test, a second is for Texas students who need to take the THEA, and a third is intended for more general use. The answer sheets are available in the back of the Lab Manual as well as report forms that foster metacognition. These report forms can be used as a portfolio activity to help assess student learning and growth. The tutorial tests appear in the Instructor's Manual that accompanies *The Effective Reader*, or you can access the tutorial tests by going to http://www.ablongman.com/henry and selecting *The Effective Reader*.

About the Series

The Skilled Reader, 3e (available in November, 2010)
The Effective Reader, 3e (available in November, 2010)
The Master Reader, 3e (available in December, 2010)

The series of skills-based textbooks, written by D. J. Henry of Daytona Beach Community College, features plentiful opportunities for students to practice individual and combined reading skills on high-interest passages from both textbooks and popular sources. Basic reading comprehension and vocabulary skills are addressed, and critical reading skills are introduced in careful step-by-step fashion.

The Henry series focuses students' attention on how their skills apply to reading college textbooks. The books also emphasize the importance of visuals, in addition to text, as valuable sources of information. Students are asked to respond to visuals throughout the series in Visual Vocabulary features. The Lab Manual offers 78 activities designed to provide additional practice and enrichment for all the topics in each book.

ABOUT THE LAB MANUAL AUTHOR

This manual is based upon much of the work of Susan Pongratz, who graduated from The College of William and Mary with a B.A. in English and an M.A. in Education. In addition to teaching developmental reading classes at Thomas Nelson Community College and co-coordinating the Verizon Reading Center there, she supervised student teachers for several years at Christopher Newport University. Since completing the Eastern Virginia Writing Project in 2002, she now serves as a teaching consultant, strongly espousing the philosophy of the reading/writing connection.

Mary Dubbé, who authored the revision of this Lab Manual, also teaches reading classes at Thomas Nelson Community College. She graduated from West Virginia University with an M.S. degree in language arts and an M.A. in reading. She has over 25 years of experience in preparing college students to be effective readers and successful students. In addition to teaching, Mary is the director of learning communities on her campus, has presented workshops at several state and national conferences, and is currently the president of the Virginia Association of Developmental Education.

Name _____ Section _____ Date _____ Score (number correct) _____ x 10 = _____

Objective: To use the SQ3R reading system to read and answer questions about the following selection from a college speech textbook.

A. Directions: Read the passage and answer the questions that follow.

Initiating Conversations

Speakers and listeners have to work together to make conversation an effective and satisfying experience. **Conversational management** includes initiating, maintaining, and closing conversations. Several approaches to initiating or opening a conversation exist. *Self-references* say something about yourself. Such references may be of the "name, rank and serial number" type—for example: "My name is Joe. I'm from Omaha." On the first day of class, students might say, "I'm worried about this class" or "I took this instructor last semester; she was excellent."

Other-references say something about the other person or ask a question: "I like that sweater." "Didn't we meet at Charlie's?" Of course, there are pitfalls here. Generally, it is best not to comment on the person's race ("My uncle married a Korean") or physical disability ("It must be awful to be confined to a wheelchair"). *Relational references* say something about the two of you: for example, "May I buy you a drink?" "Would you like to dance?" or simply, "May I join you?" *Context references* say something about the physical, social, cultural, or temporal context. The familiar, "Do you have the time?" is a reference of this type. But you can be more creative and say, for example, "This restaurant seems very friendly," or "This Dalí is fantastic."
    —Adapted from De Vito, *The Interpersonal Communication Book,* 10th ed., p. 218.

_____ 1. While surveying this article, the effective reader would first notice _____.
      a. the questions in the 2nd paragraph
      b. the examples of approaches to initiate conversation
      c. the word *references* within both paragraphs
      d. the phrases in bold print and in italics

_____ 2. Which of the following would be helpful to know prior to reading this article?
      a. background about Korea
      b. an explanation of the word *references*
      c. background about Charlie's
      d. information about common disabilities

_____ 3. Which of the following questions will help the effective reader focus on the main ideas of this article?
      a. What is a Dalí?
      b. What are some tips to overcome shyness?
      c. How can conversation be managed?
      d. Where are the best places to meet interesting people?

_____4. According to the information in the first paragraph, *self-references* _____.
     a. ask questions about the listener
     b. ask questions about the location
     c. are comments about the person in charge
     d. are personal comments about oneself

_____5. The phrase *other-references* in the second paragraph most likely means _____.
     a. research material
     b. former employers who can vouch for one's work history
     c. literary works
     d. statements or questions that refer to the listener

_____6. An example of a *context reference* is _____.
     a. "The lead singer of this band is from Haiti."
     b. "Have you heard this band before today?"
     c. "I like your taste in music."
     d. "This is the tenth time I have listened to this group perform."

_____7. Which of the following questions concerning this passage would most likely appear on a test?
     a. Explain the term conversational management.
     b. Define the term *self-reference* and give an example.
     c. What is the difference between a *relational reference* and an *other-reference*?
     d. All of the above

B. Directions: Read this passage and answer the following questions.

Poor health can result from any of three main types of malnutrition. One type, **undernutrition,** is an inadequate intake of energy. In some parts of the world, it is *endemic* (common throughout a region for many years) because of wars, floods, droughts, or farming practices that make widespread crop failure common. Undernourished adults and children appear **wasted**, with a low body weight for their height. Children who do not eat enough food to support their growth are often shorter than would be expected for their age, a condition known as **stunting**. In circumstances of extreme hunger, children can be both stunted and wasted.
     —Adapted from Thompson and Manore, *Nutrition for Life*, 2nd ed., p. 410.

_____8. Which of the following questions most effectively reflects the main idea of this passage?
     a. Where does malnutrition occur?
     b. How serious of a problem is malnutrition?
     c. What is one type of malnutrition?
     d. Why do people have poor health, given the advances of modern science and medicine?

_____9. According to the context, *endemic* means _____.
     a. rare
     b. widespread
     c. of poor quality
     d. irrelevant

_____10. What kind of information should the effective reader expect to see next?
    a.   information about third world countries
    b.   information about corruption within charitable organizations that supply food
    c.   information about two other types of malnutrition
    d.   information about other causes of poor health

Name_____Section _____ Date _____ Score (number correct) _____ x 10 = _____

Objective: To use the SQ3R reading system to read a selection from a college psychology textbook.

Directions: Read the following excerpt and answer the questions that follow.

Primacy and Recency Effects

1 In a typical memory experiment, a participant may be asked to study a list of words and recall as many of the items as possible so that the researcher can determine whether the information was transferred from short-term memory storage to long-term memory. If the list is 30 or 40 items long, such experiments typically show an overall recall rate of 20%, but memory is not even throughout the list. Recall is higher for words at the beginning of a series than for those in the middle, a phenomenon termed the **primacy effect**. This effect occurs because no information related to the task at hand is already stored in short-term storage; at the moment a person begins a new task, attention to new stimuli is at its peak. In addition, words at the beginning of a series get to be rehearsed more often, allowing them to be transferred to long-term memory. Thus, the primacy effect is associated with long-term memory processes.

2 However, recall is even higher for words at the end of the series—a phenomenon termed the **recency effect**. These more recently presented items are still being held in short-term storage, where they can be actively rehearsed without interference as they are encoded for long-term memory. The recency effect is thus thought to be related to short-term storage.

3 When one item on a list differs from the others—for example, an adjective in a series of common nouns or a longer word in a series of short ones—the one different item is learned more easily. This is the phenomenon called the **von Restorff effect**.

—Adapted from Lefton & Brannon, *Psychology*, 8th ed., pp. 283–285.

_____1. When skimming the title and first paragraph, an effective reader would ask all of the following *except* _____.
   a. What does the word *primacy* mean?
   b. What does the word *recency* mean?
   c. What do I already know about sociology?
   d. What do I already know about short-term memory?

_____2. A question the reader would formulate while skimming the passage would include all of the following *except* _____.
   a. What is the primacy effect?
   b. What is the recency effect?
   c. What is the von Restorff effect?
   d. Who conducts research on memory?

_____3. Which line would an active learner probably highlight as a main idea?
   a. In a typical memory experiment, a participant may be asked to study a list of words and recall as many of the items as possible so that the researcher can determine whether the information transferred from short-term storage to long-term memory.
   b. If the list is 30 to 40 items long, such experiments typically show an overall recall rate of 20%, but memory is not even throughout the list.
   c. Recall is higher for words at the beginning of a series than for those in the middle, a phenomenon termed the **primacy effect**.
   d. The primacy effect is associated with long-term memory.

_____4. In paragraph 2, the word _phenomenon_ probably means _____.
   a. sight
   b. organization
   c. experience
   d. noun

_____5. Which of the following would an effective reader highlight in this passage?
   a. the entire first paragraph
   b. the examples provided in paragraph 3
   c. the bold-faced words and their definitions
   d. all of the last paragraph

_____6. Questions an active learner might pose as he or she skims the material would include all of the following _except_ _____.
   a. How can the von Restorff effect help in my own study routine?
   b. Would studying in smaller chunks of time with short breaks in between help me to improve my memory?
   c. What should I do on my study breaks?
   d. How can perceptual imagery help me in my studies?

_____7. According to the context, the best definition of _recall_ is _____.
   a. a request to return something
   b. dismiss from office
   c. resemble something
   d. remember something

_____8. From this article, the effective reader could assume that _____.
   a. the beginning of a list is the most difficult part to recall
   b. the middle of a list is the most difficult part to recall
   c. the end of a list is the most difficult part to recall
   d. placement in a list has no effect on ability to recall

_____9. The _von Restorff effect_ concludes that _____.
   a. a differing item in a series is easier to remember
   b. similar items in a series are easier to remember
   c. items in a series are nearly impossible to remember
   d. things that are similar are easier to remember than things that are different

5

_____10. Which sentence best summarizes this article?
     a. Experiments show that the recall average of a list is 20%.
     b. The primacy effect is a phenomenon that emerges in memory research.
     c. Experiments show that many variables can affect one's ability to recall items in a list.
     d. Memory is often a subject explored by researchers.

Name_____ Section _____ Date _____ Score (number correct) _____ x 10 = _____

Directions: Use effective reading skills to answer the questions that follow this passage.

Students Sing the Blues

Campus Blues

1 The stressors of college life, such as anxiety over relationships, pressure to get good grades and win social acceptance, abuse of alcohol and other drugs, poor diet, and lack of sleep can create a <u>toxic</u> cocktail. It is no surprise that depression on college campuses is a huge problem. According to a longitudinal study of students who sought help at campus over a 13-year period, sources of depression changed from relationship and money problems in the 1980s to more serious forms of stress-related anxiety in later years, paralleling trends in society as a whole.

2 International students are particularly <u>vulnerable</u> to mental health concerns. Being far from home without the security of family and friends can <u>exacerbate</u> problems and make coping difficult. Most campuses have cultural centers and other services available; however, many students do not utilize them.

Treating Depression

3 The best treatment involves determining the person's type and degree of depression and its possible causes. Both psychotherapeutic and pharmacological modes of treatment are recommended for clinical (severe and prolonged) depression. Drugs often relieve the symptoms of depression, such as loss of sleep or appetite, while psychotherapy can be equally helpful for improving the ability to function. In some cases, psychotherapy alone may be the most successful treatment. The most common psychotherapeutic treatments for depression are **cognitive therapy** and **interpersonal therapy.**

—Donatelle, *Access to Health*, 10th ed., p. 59.

_____1.   While surveying this article, what should an effective reader first notice?
      a.   the words *psychotherapeutic* and *pharmacological*
      b.   the references to numbers: *13-year period* and *1980s*
      c.   the bold-faced heading **Treating Depression** and the bold-faced words in the last paragraph
      d.   the name of the author

_____2. An effective reader might first think this article focuses on the music genre, the blues. What adjustment will the reader make after completing the survey?
   a. The reader will realize this is the correct topic.
   b. The reader will realize this article is about depression among college students and recommended ways to treat it.
   c. The reader will understand that this article is a humorous description of campus life.
   d. The reader will realize that the focus of this article is on the definition of therapy.

_____3. All of the following questions will help the effective reader focus on the main ideas of this article *except* _____.
   a. What causes stress among college students?
   b. How is depression treated?
   c. Which college major causes the highest levels of stress in students?
   d. What do cognitive therapy and interpersonal therapy mean?

_____4. This article suggests that _____.
   a. All students are equally at risk for depression.
   b. International students are more at risk for mental-health concerns than American students.
   c. College life has become much less stressful over the years.
   d. Lack of sleep is the most common reason for stress in college students.

_____5. Upon examining the way *toxic* is used in paragraph 1, which educated guess should the effective reader make about the meaning of a *toxic cocktail*?
   a. a dangerous alcoholic drink
   b. a harmful combination of things that cause stress
   c. a poisonous substance
   d. a contaminating pollutant

_____6. What is the most likely definition of *vulnerable* in paragraph 2?
   a. resistant
   b. fortified
   c. at risk
   d. closed

_____7. The word *exacerbate* in paragraph 2 most likely means _____.
   a. improve
   b. move out
   c. inform
   d. worsen

_____8. What logical conclusion can the effective reader make about a clinical depression from this article? A clinical depression is _____.
   a. an unemotional illness
   b. a low-pressure area
   c. an experimental design
   d. a long-term and serious psychological disorder

_____9. A pharmacological mode of treating depression would most likely involve the use of
   a. prescription drugs.
   b. journal writing.
   c. talking with a counselor.
   d. upbeat music.

_____10. Which sentence best summarizes the main ideas of this selection?
   a. Depression among college students is increasing, but there are effective treatments for this mental health disorder.
   b. Psychotherapy is an effective way to treat depression among college students.
   c. Depression is a serious mental health disorder.
   d. International students are particularly vulnerable to depression.

9

Name_____ Section _____ Date _____ Score (number correct) _____ x 10 = _____

Directions: Use effective reading skills to answer the questions that follow this passage.

Violence against Women

1 In the nineteenth century, men claimed the right to rule their households, even to the point of using physical discipline against their wives, and a great deal of "manly" violence is still directed at women. A government report estimates that 587,000 aggravated assaults against women occur annually. To this number can be added 233,000 rapes or sexual assaults and perhaps 1.8 million simple assaults (U.S. Department of Justice, 2008).

2 *Gender violence* is also an issue on college and university campuses. According to research carried out by the U.S. Department of Justice, in a given academic year, about 3 percent of female college students become victims of rape. Projecting these figures over a typical five-year college career, about 20 percent of college women experience rape. In 90 percent of all cases the victim knew the offender, and most of the assaults took place in the woman's living quarters (Karjane, Fisher, & Cullen, 2005)

3 Off campus, most gender-linked violence also occurs where most interaction between women and men takes place: in the home. Richard Gelles (cited in Roesch, 1984) argues that with the exception of the police and the military, the family is the most violent organization in the United States, and women suffer most of the injuries. The risk of violence is especially great for low-income women living in families that face a great deal of stress; low-income women also have fewer options to get out of a dangerous home.

4 Violence against women also occurs in casual relationships. Ironically, most rapes involve men known, and often trusted, by the victims. Dianne Herman (2001) claims that abuse of women is built into our way of life. All forms of violence against women—from the catcalls that intimidate women on city streets to a pinch in a crowded subway to physical assaults that occur at home—express what she calls a "*rape culture*" of men trying to dominate women. Sexual violence is fundamentally about power, not sex, and therefore should be understood as a dimension of *gender stratification*.
                              —Adapted from Macionis, *Sociology*, 13th ed., p. 340.

_____1. While surveying this article, the effective reader would first notice _____.
      a.   the reasons why women are assaulted
      b.   the research studies that are quoted
      c.   information from the U.S. Department of Justice
      d.   the heading and the phrase *gender violence*

_____2. Which of the following would be helpful to know prior to reading this article?
      a.   the statistics for violence against men
      b.   ways of relieving stress in a family
      c.   the definition of the term *gender*
      d.   research studies about successful women

_____3. Which of the following questions will help the effective reader focus upon the main ideas of this selection?
   a. What types of violence are directed primarily at women?
   b. How is research about women's issues conducted?
   c. Where can information be found from the Department of Justice?
   d. When does the Department of Justice release its statistics?

_____4. According to the information in this passage, which of the following statements is true?
   a. Low-income wives now have many options to help them leave a dangerous home.
   b. "Manly" violence is necessary to keep women in their place.
   c. About one-fifth of female college students will experience rape over a five-year period.
   d. Strangers cause most violence against women.

_____5. According to context in paragraph four, "rape culture" can best be defined as _____.
   a. a society that permits rape
   b. a custom of tolerating male aggression toward women
   c. a view that wives are property owned by their husbands
   d. a tradition of hatred toward women

_____6. Which information will help the effective reader better understand the ideas in paragraph four?
   a. reasons why men pinch women
   b. background information about Dianne Herman
   c. the definition of _gender stratification_
   d. why women have casual relationships

_____7. From this article, the effective reader could assume that _____.
   a. gender violence toward women is often caused by the need to overpower and dominate
   b. gender violence will never be punished
   c. statistics from the Department of Justice are probably skewed in favor of men
   d. men no longer have the right to govern their households

B. Directions: Read this passage and answer the following questions.

Energy Conservation Has Followed Economic Need

1 In the United States, many people first saw the value of conserving energy following the OPEC embargo of 1973–1974. Conservation measures enacted by the U.S. government in response to that event included a mandated increase in the miles-per-gallon (mpg) fuel efficiency of automobiles and a reduction in the national speed limit to 55 miles per hour.

2 Over the past three decades, however, many of these initiatives were abandoned. Without high market prices and an immediate threat of shortages, people lacked economic motivation to conserve. Government funding for research into alternative energy sources decreased, speed limits increased, and U.S. policy makers repeatedly failed to raise the corporate average fuel efficiency (CAFE) standards, which set benchmarks for auto manufacturers to meet.

11

3 At last, Congress passed legislation in 2007 mandating that automakers raise average fuel efficiency to 35 mpg by the year 2020. This is a substantial advance, yet even after this boost, American automobiles will still lag behind the efficiency of the vehicles of most other developed nations For instance, the fuel efficiency of European and Japanese cars is nearly twice that of U.S. cars and is slated to keep improving.

—Adapted from Withgott and Brennan, *Essential Environment: The Science Behind the Stories*, 3rd ed., p. 343.

_____8. Which of the following questions most effectively reflects the main idea of this passage?
- a. What are our country's energy problems?
- b. When was the OPEC embargo?
- c. How has energy conservation followed economic need in the United States?
- d. Why do people buy cars that have low gas mileage?

_____9. What background knowledge might help the reader better understand the ideas in this article?
- a. a list of car manufacturers in the United States
- b. pictures of cars manufactured overseas
- c. an explanation of how car engines work
- d. information about the OPEC embargo of 1973–1974

_____10. According to the information in paragraph two, CAFE most likely is _____.
- a. Corporate Average Fuel Economy, the required average fuel economy for a vehicle manufacturer's fleet of vehicles for each model year
- b. Comparative Aircraft Flight Efficiency, a research company that tests and evaluates small aircraft
- c. Compatible Automotive Ford Equivalents, a company that finds off-brand parts for Ford vehicles
- d. Comprehensive Automotive Factory Enforcements, a company that provides reinforcing products that make cars more durable

Name_____ Section _____ Date _____ Score (number correct) _____ x 10 = _____

Directions: Read the passage and answer the questions that follow.

1 Having lampooned the Eisenhower administration as <u>stodgy</u> and unimaginative, President Kennedy made a show of his style and wit. He <u>flouted</u> convention by naming his younger brother Robert attorney general. "I can't see that it's wrong to give him a little legal experience before he goes out to practice law," the president quipped. Kennedy also prided himself on being a man of letters, winner of the Pulitzer Prize for *Profiles in Courage*. He quoted Robert Frost and Dante. He played and replayed recordings of Winston Churchill, hoping to imprint the great orator's sonorous cadences on his own flat Bostonian vowels. At the instigation of his elegant wife, Jacqueline, Kennedy surrounded himself with the finest intellects at glittering White House <u>galas</u> to honor Nobel Prize winners and celebrated artists.

2 Kennedy's youthful senior staff boasted impressive scholarly credentials. His national security advisor, McGeorge Bundy, had been dean of the faculty at Harvard (and the first undergraduate at Yale to receive perfect scores in three college entrance examinations). Secretary of Defense Robert McNamara also had taught at Harvard before becoming the first non-family member to head the Ford Motor Company. The administration constituted, as journalist David Halberstam observed later, somewhat ruefully, "the best and the brightest."

3 Kennedy's campaign slogan—"Let's get this country moving again"—was embodied in his own active life. He played rugged games of touch football with the press corps and romped with his young children in the Oval Office. In an article for *Sports Illustrated* entitled "The Soft American" and published just after the election, Kennedy complained that television, movies, and a comfortable lifestyle had made too many young people flabby. His earliest presidential initiative was a physical fitness campaign in the schools.

4 Kennedy's image of youthful vigor ("vigah," as he pronounced the word) was enhanced by the beauty and presence of Jacqueline, whose wide-eyed diffidence was commonly misunderstood and universally admired as regal bearing. The image was enhanced by Lerner and Loew's musical *Camelot*, which opened a few weeks before the inauguration. Its evocation of King Arthur, who sought to lead his virile young knights in challenges of great and good, suggested the Kennedy White House. (The musical became a favorite of the president; he often listened to the cast recordings before going to sleep.) All Washington seemed aglow with excitement and energy. In the words of the administration's chief chronicler, Arthur M. Schlesinger Jr. (another former Harvard professor): "Never had girls seemed so pretty, tunes so melodious, and evenings so blithe and unconstrained."

5 Never, too, had the substance of an administration been so closely identified with the style of its president. But the dazzle was misleading. Although quick-witted and intelligent, Kennedy was no intellectual. His favorite reading was the James Bond spy novels of Ian Fleming. He never admitted it publicly, but most of *Profiles of Courage* had been ghostwritten by paid writers.

13

6 Nor did the president embody physical fitness. Congenital back problems, aggravated by war injuries, forced Kennedy to use crutches or a cane in private and to take heavy doses of painkillers and amphetamines. The president's permanent "tan" did not result from outdoor exercise, as the public assumed, but from Addison's disease, an often fatal failure of the adrenal glands for which Kennedy gave himself daily injections of cortisone. Though he publicly denied it, Kennedy was chronically ill throughout his presidency.

—Adapted from Carnes & Garraty, *The American Nation,* 11th ed., pp. 789–90.

____1.   Which question would an effective reader ask while reading this passage?
    a.   Who was the president of France during Kennedy's administration?
    b.   Which of President Kennedy's brothers is currently a U.S. senator?
    c.   What do I already know about President Kennedy?
    d.   Where was Kennedy born?

____2. Which question would be helpful for an effective reader to consider while reading this passage?
    a.   What do I know about the play *Camelot* and the outcome of King Arthur?
    b.   How many members of Kennedy's staff attended Harvard University?
    c.   What other magazines did Kennedy read besides *Sports Illustrated*?
    d.   What were Kennedy's favorite TV shows?

____3. According to the context of paragraph 1, the best definition of *stodgy* is _____.
    a.   cheerful
    b.   creative
    c.   dull and boring
    d.   inspiring enthusiasm

____4. According to the context of paragraph 1, the best definition of *flouted* is _____.
    a.   mocked
    b.   obeyed
    c.   created
    d.   followed

____5. According to the context of paragraph 1, the best definition of *galas* is _____.
    a.   public tours
    b.   work sessions
    c.   festive occasions
    d.   camping trips

____6.   Which mental picture would an effective reader create while reading paragraph 3?
    a.   Kennedy playing touch football
    b.   Kennedy watching TV and eating pork rinds
    c.   Kennedy watching movies and eating popcorn
    d.   Kennedy napping in the Oval Office

____7.   Which mental picture would an effective reader create while reading paragraph 6?
    a.   Kennedy in a hospital bed
    b.   Knights in armor and beautiful women
    c.   Studious scholars in dimly lit libraries
    d.   Long lines at the gas pumps

14

____8. Which is the best restatement of paragraph 2?

    a. Kennedy's staff was comprised of some of the country's most intellectually elite, who had proved their success in other venues.

    b. Most of Kennedy's staff members were too young to serve in the difficult positions in which they had been appointed.

    c. While he was very bright, Secretary of Defense Robert McNamara should have stayed at the Ford Motor Company.

    d. Though very bright, many of Kennedy's staff members did not have enough government experience to serve the country's best interests.

____9. Which is the best restatement of paragraph 3?

    a. Kennedy was responsible for the establishment of MTV.

    b. Kennedy was a strong critic of the film industry.

    c. Kennedy was concerned that the country's students were spending too much time in front of the television and not enough time in our nation's libraries.

    d. Kennedy was concerned that young people were becoming less active, so one of his first accomplishments was his school physical fitness campaign.

____10. What is the best restatement of paragraphs 5–6?

    a. Kennedy was largely responsible for the popularity of the James Bond films.

    b. Much of what the public saw in President Kennedy was based on the image he presented rather than the reality that existed.

    c. The president was not as physically fit as he was portrayed by the press.

    d. Though a well-kept secret, a chronic illness plagued the president.

Name _____ Section _____ Date _____ Score (number correct) _____ x 10 = _____

Directions: Read the complete sociology section and answer the questions that follow.

Marriage and Family in Global Perspective

1 To better understand U.S. patterns of marriage and family, let's first look at how customs differ around the world. This will give us a context for interpreting our own experiences in this vital social institution.

What Is a Family?

2 "What is a family, anyway?" asked William Sayres (1992) at the beginning of an article on this topic. By this question, he meant that although the family is so significant to humanity that it is <u>universal</u>— every human group in the world organizes its members in families—the world's cultures display so much variety that the term *family* is difficult to define. For example, although the Western world regards a family as a husband, wife, and children, other groups have family forms in which men have more than one wife (**polygyny**) or women more than one husband (**polyandry**). How about the obvious? Can we define family as the approved group into which children are born? This would overlook the Banaro of New Guinea. In this group, a young woman must give birth before she can marry—and she *cannot* marry the father of her child (Murdock 1949).

3 And so it goes. For just about every element you might regard as essential to marriage or family, some group has a different custom. Consider the sex of the bride and groom. Although in almost every instance the bride and groom are female and male, there are exceptions. In some Native American tribes, a man or woman who wanted to be a member of the opposite sex went through a ceremony (*berdache*) and was declared a member of the opposite sex. Not only did the "new" man or woman do the tasks associated with his or her new sex, but also the individual was allowed to marry. In this instance, the husband and wife were of the same biological sex. In the contemporary world, Denmark (in 1989), Norway (in 1993), Sweden (in 1995), and Holland (in 1998) have legalized same-sex marriages.

—Henslin, *Essentials of Sociology*, 5th ed., pp. 324–326.

_____1.	After surveying the title, headings, and first paragraph, which would an effective reader anticipate to follow?

    a.	reasons people choose to marry
    b.	the history of marriage and how it has changed over time
    c.	the definition of marriage and family and the role culture plays in each
    d.	a comparison of American families past and present

16

_____2. Questions a student might form after surveying and before reading this passage would include all of the following *except*
   a. What is family?
   b. What kind of person would make a good spouse?
   c. How might a global perspective of family differ from what I already know?
   d. Are families the same in all cultures?

_____3. According to the context of paragraph 1, the best definition of *universal* is _____.
   a. important
   b. mandatory
   c. world-wide
   d. optional

_____4. According to the context of paragraph 2, *polygyny* means _____.
   a. having more than one husband
   b. having more than one wife
   c. marrying outside one's faith
   d. marrying outside one's tribe

_____5. According to the context of paragraph 2, *polyandry* means _____.
   a. having more than one husband
   b. having more than one wife
   c. marrying outside one's faith
   d. marrying outside one's tribe

_____6. According to the context of paragraph 2, a *berdache* is a Native American _____.
   a. spouse
   b. dwelling
   c. ceremony
   d. healer

_____7. Marriage among the Banaro in New Guinea depends upon _____.
   a. the ability of the wife to have children
   b. the ability of the husband to provide for a family
   c. the amount of the dowry provided by the bride's father
   d. the approval of the new mother-in-law by the husband's family

_____8. Based on the information in paragraph 3, marriage customs _____.
   a. are the same around the word
   b. prevent same-sex marriages around the world
   c. differ around the word
   d. stem from political views

_____9. Which sentence in paragraph 3 should an effective reader highlight?
   a. And so it goes.
   b. For just about every element you might regard as essential to marriage . . .
   c. Consider the sex of the bride and groom.
   d. Although in almost every instance the bride and groom are male and female, . . .

17

____10. Which one of the following sentences best summarizes this article?
    a. Families are significant to humanity.
    b. Groups around the world have different customs.
    c. We can define family as the approved group into which children are born.
    d. The concept of family is universal but is difficult to define because of differing cultural views around the world.

Name _____ Section _____ Date _____ Score (number correct) _____ x 10 = _____

Directions: Using the context clues and your knowledge of word parts, select the best definition for the word in **bold** print.

Read the excerpt "Personal Space," from a college psychology textbook. Then respond to the items that follow it.

Personal Space

To help **assert** their individuality and **maintain** a sense of personal control, human beings generally try to establish appropriate degrees of personal space. **Personal space** is the area around an individual that the person considers private and that is **enclosed** by an invisible psychological boundary. **Encroachment** on that space causes displeasure and often withdrawal.

The size of your personal space can change, depending on the situation and the people near you. For example, you may walk arm in arm with a family member, but you will avoid physical contact with a stranger. You may stand close to a friend and whisper in her ear, but you will keep a certain distance from an elevator operator or a store clerk.

Anthropologist Edward Hall suggested that personal space is a **mechanism** by which people communicate with others. He **proposed** that people **adhere** to established norms of personal space that are learned in childhood. Hall observed that the use of personal space also varies from culture to culture. In the United States, especially in suburban and rural areas, people are used to large homes and generous personal space. In Japan, on the other hand, people are used to small homes that provide little personal space. In general, Western cultures insist on a fair amount of space for people, reserving **proximity** for intimacy and close friends, while Arab and some Eastern cultures allow much smaller distances between strangers.

Of course, determining personal space is a tricky **endeavor**, and researchers are trying to sort out distance estimations for adults and children and for men and women.

—Adapted from Lefton and Brannon, *Psychology,* 8th ed., pp. 635–636.

_____1. **Assert** means _____.
    a. deny
    b. declare
    c. lessen
    d. increase

_____2. **Maintain** means _____.
    a. keep in a certain place or condition
    b. plan for future use
    c. show a cooperative spirit
    d. eliminate competition

19

_____3. As used in the passage, "the area around an individual that the person considers private and that is enclosed by an individual psychological boundary" is known as _____.
- a. social distance
- b. spatial zones
- c. public zone
- d. personal space

_____4. **Enclosed** means _____.
- a. surrounded
- b. subdued
- c. opened
- d. withdrawn

_____5. **Encroachment** means _____.
- a. movement
- b. confusion
- c. intrusion
- d. encounter

_____6. **Mechanism** means _____.
- a. machinery
- b. system
- c. substance
- d. means

_____7. **Proposed** means _____.
- a. promised
- b. wrote
- c. vowed
- d. suggested

_____8. **Adhere** means _____.
- a. give up
- b. change
- c. hold on to
- d. advance

_____9. **Proximity** means _____.
- a. sympathy
- b. distance
- c. nearness.
- d. failure

_____10. **Endeavor** means _____.
- a. undertaking
- b. path
- c. experiment
- d. illusion

20

Name_____ Section _____ Date _____ Score (number correct) _____ x 10 = _____

Objective: To determine the definitions of unfamiliar words by using context clues.

Directions: Using the context clues and your knowledge of word parts, select the best definition for the word in **bold** print.

1. Alison knew she was **obsessed** with her fear of failure, so she read several self-help books to learn how to stop her constant negative self-talk.
    a. hidden in a dark corner
    b. haunted by a particular thought explained
    c. overcome with sudden joy
    d. provided with a particular talent

2. People who lead a **sedentary** life—that is, those who sit all day at their jobs and then at home—are encouraged by physicians to find ways to introduce some exercise into their daily routine.
    a. consisting of a layer of rock and sand
    b. aided by an assistant
    c. privately arranged
    d. characterized by little physical activity

3. As the college seniors lined up for the graduation ceremony, they grew **wistful**, sharing memories of the past four years and already longing for the simple, predictable days of attending classes.
    a. full of yearning or longing for something
    b. lacking thought or care
    c. sneaking an opportunity to change plans
    d. secretly planning a new move

4. **Impulsive** shoppers rarely think about the consequences of making large credit card purchases.
    a. deliberately denying oneself a present
    b. planning with great preparation
    c. logically weighing the possible consequences of an action
    d. acting without thought of the future

5. All students are expected to **adhere** to classroom rules; for those who do not stick to the codes set by the college, there will be negative consequences.
    a. celebrate
    b. follow
    c. begin a new journey
    d. deliberately avoid punishment

21

6.   Although the **diminutive** speaker had to stand on a box to be seen over the lectern, the audience agreed that his ideas were anything but small.
       a.   unusually tall
       b.   intelligent
       c.   distinguished
       d.   short or small

7.   The two-year-old was **reluctant** to get his first haircut until he saw the smiling stylist dressed as a kind fairy godmother.
       a.   willing and eager
       b.   sensitive
       c.   unwilling and resistant
       d.   remarkable and superior

_____8.   Why is it that strange people who are rich are considered **eccentric**, but strange poor people are merely odd?
       a.   sad
       b.   inexpensive
       c.   ordinary
       d.   unusual

_____9.   Wearing **conventional** clothes to a job interview at a bank is highly recommended, whereas more unusual outfits are acceptable for individuals seeking jobs as entertainers and artists.
       a.   having to do with a conference
       b.   customary and usual
       c.   unusual
       d.   expensive

_____10. Despite the onset of Alzheimer's disease, the patient had some good days when he was **cognizant** of his surroundings and aware of the loved ones who visited him.
       a.   forgetful
       b.   healthy
       c.   aware
       d.   angry

22

Name_____ Section _____ Date _____ Score (number correct) _____ x 10 = _____

A. Directions: Using the context clues and your knowledge of word parts, select the best definition for the word in **bold** print.

1.   Rose is neither loud nor outgoing; instead, she is **introverted**.
        a. quiet and withdrawn
        b. mean or aggressive
        c. strong-willed
        d. intelligent

2.   Many forms of cancer can remain **latent** for years before they develop active symptoms that demand treatment.
        a. dangerous
        b. harmless
        c. inactive
        d. localized

3.   Racing legend Dale Earnhardt earned the nickname "The **Intimidator**" because he was known for bumping the cars of other racers to frighten them out of the way during a race.
        a. fool
        b. bully
        c. champion
        d. father

4.   Completing homework and projects on time, attending class, and taking notes are all **conducive** to academic success.
        a. barriers
        b. unfavorable
        c. helpful
        d. steps

5.   Countless young people have traveled to Hollywood to escape their **mundane,** ordinary lives.
        a. routine
        b. confused
        c. exciting
        d. carefree

6.   Marcel spat out his anger in a few **curt** words that cut deeply into Ashleigh's feelings.
        a. humorous
        b. sharp
        c. forgetful
        d. admirable

23

7.   As I rolled up my car window, the traffic noise was **muted**, and I could better hear the music on my favorite CD.
    a. hushed
    b. loud
    c. blaring
    d. horrible

8.   The thief's alibi for the time of the crime was **implausible**; he said he was at work, yet police knew he had been fired from that job two days earlier.
    a. forgiven
    b. humorous
    c. unbelievable
    d. interesting

B. Directions: Use the context clues and your knowledge of word parts in the following passage to determine the best meaning of the underlined words.

The hidden self contains all that you know of yourself and of others that you keep secret. In any <u>interaction</u>, this area includes everything you don't want to reveal, whether it's relevant or irrelevant to the conversation. At the extremes we have the <u>overdisclosers</u> and the underdisclosers. The overdisclosers tell all. They tell you their marital difficulties, their children's problems, their financial status, and just about everything else. The underdisclosers tell nothing. They talk abut you but not about themselves.

—Adapted from DeVito, *The Interpersonal Communication Book*, 11th ed. p. 59.

9.   The best definition of *interaction* is _____.
    a. business
    b. building
    c. argument
    d. communication

10.   The best definition of *overdisclosers* is _____.
    a. those revealing too many private details
    b. those revealing too few private details
    c. those hiding personal information
    d. those capable of running great distances

Name_____ Section _____ Date _____ Score (number correct) _____ x 10 = _____

A. Directions: Using the context clues and your knowledge of word parts, select the best definition for the word in **bold** print.

_____1. Peanut, a cross between a poodle and a Chihuahua, is a **bizarre** or weird-looking dog.
     a. strange
     b. cute
     c. small
     d. ordinary

_____2. Rita is not dishonest or hypocritical; in fact, the consistency of her beliefs, words, and actions makes her highly **credible**.
     a. unbelievable
     b. amazing
     c. believable
     d. susceptible

_____3. My brother's **charisma** makes him extremely popular and influential.
     a. wealth
     b. appeal
     c. education
     d. political power

_____4. During the trial, three witnesses were asked to **attest** to the defendant's whereabouts during the time the murder took place.
     a. disprove
     b. discuss
     c. challenge
     d. confirm

_____5. Former first lady Laura Bush, as a previous teacher and librarian, is a **proponent** of literacy.
     a. rival
     b. supporter
     c. doubter
     d. judge

_____6. If a blister **ruptures**, do not remove the broken skin covering it unless the skin is dirty; wash the area with soap and water and smooth the skin flap over the tender area.
     a. appears
     b. disappears
     c. bursts
     d. explodes

25

B. Directions: Study the following word chart. Then match the word to its definition using word parts and context clues.

Prefix	Meaning	Root	Meaning	Suffix	Meaning
dis-	down, away	*loc*	place	*-ate*	cause
re-	again back	*pater*	father	*-al*	of, like, related to
		aster	star	*-oid*	In the form of

_____7. Scientists have long thought that a giant _____ collided with earth and wiped out the dinosaurs.
   a. paternal
   b. asteroid
   c. relocate
   d. dislocated

_____8. Family leave laws give men the right to take _____ leaves from their jobs so that they may care for and bond with their newborn children.
   a. paternal
   b. asteroid
   c. relocate
   d. dislocated

_____9. Large companies often expect their employees to _____ to an office in another city or state in order to move up the corporate ladder.
   a. paternal
   b. asteroid
   c. relocate
   d. dislocated

_____10. As Jeremy's _____ shoulder was put back in its socket by the doctor, he winced with pain.
   a. paternal
   b. asteroid
   c. relocate
   d. dislocated

Name_____ Section _____ Date _____ Score (number correct) _____ x 10 = _____

A. Directions: Using context clues and your knowledge of word parts, choose the best meaning for each of the words in **bold** type.

1. Exercise, proper diet, and regular medical exams may increase one's **longevity** or life span.
   a. height
   b. muscle mass
   c. length of life
   d. quality of life

2. Marty broke up with Marie because he said she **hampered** his ability to feel good about himself.
   a. increased
   b. blocked
   c. supported
   d. created

3. Some songs from the 1960s and 1970s bring back **poignant**—emotional—memories of good times from my late teenage years.
   a. bitter
   b. hurtful
   c. unlikely
   d. touching

4. Obesity is no longer rare among American youth. It has become alarmingly **prevalent**.
   a. uncommon
   b. purposeful
   c. overweight
   d. widespread

5. Because Joshua did not plan to give his speech today, he had to **improvise** his presentation.
   a. quickly create
   b. avoid giving
   c. carefully prepare
   d. accept failure for

6. Colin faced a **dilemma** when his car wouldn't start on the very morning he had his job interview.
   a. question
   b. solution
   c. problem
   d. benefit

27

_____7. Education offers people skills and knowledge and acts as a **deterrent** of crime and poverty.
     a. help
     b. something that prevents
     c. waste
     d. benefit

_____8. Ordinarily a little plump, Margaret's **gaunt** appearance shocked her family.
     a. healthy and fit
     b. happy
     c. thin and bony
     d. strong

B. Directions: Use the context clues and your knowledge of word parts in the following passage to determine the best meaning of the underlined words.

The Amazon story is underline{emblematic} of the e-commerce environment of the past ten years: an early period of business vision, inspiration, and experimentation, followed by the realization that establishing a successful business would not be easy. Consequently, Jeff Bezos, the creator, had to underline{retrench} and reevaluate his plan. The changes he made ultimately led to a more finely tuned business model that actually produces profits.

            —Adapted from Laudon and Traver, *E-commerce,* 3rd ed., p. 139.

_____9. The best definition of *emblematic* is _____.
     a. representative
     b. non-characteristic
     c. unbelievable
     d. measurable

_____10. The best definition of *retrench* is _____.
     a. expand
     b. rethink
     c. walk back
     d. resist

Name_____ Section _____ Date _____ Score (number correct) _____ x 10 = _____

A. Directions: Using context clues and your knowledge of word parts, choose the best meaning for each of the words in **bold** type.

1. Many famous and wealthy people use their power and position for **altruistic** rather than selfish causes.
    a. sharp
    b. charitable
    c. political
    d. greedy

2. The vice president of the United States has the power to cast a tie-breaking vote when the Senate reaches an **impasse** on passing a bill, resolution, or law.
    a. agreement
    b. standoff
    c. dialogue
    d. amendment

3. The **epigraph** written on the cornerstone of the library building read, "In dedication to the vision and heart of Beverly Statton."
    a. newspaper
    b. journal
    c. inscription
    d. sculpture

4. Politicians pay special attention to **demographic** information such as the age, gender, and income levels of the citizens in their voting districts.
    a. statistics of the human population
    b. financial information about a city
    c. medical information about a group of people
    d. religious information about a group of citizens

5. Every flu season, health experts work to avoid an **epidemic** of influenza.
    a. opportunity
    b. occupation
    c. outbreak
    d. opening

6. Cartoonists make a living using their **graphic** skills to amuse audiences.
    a. mediocre
    b. architectural
    c. masonry
    d. drawing

29

7. One form of peer pressure is the act of **shunning** an individual who seems different by making that person feel isolated and alone.
    a. praising
    b. accepting
    c. rejecting
    d. insulting

8. Robert rarely saves his money; instead, he **squanders** every penny on entertainment and clothes.
    a. wastes
    b. saves
    c. invests
    d. consumes

B. Directions: Use the context clues and your knowledge of word parts in the following passage to determine the best meaning of the underlined words.

The ability to control behavior is important because it gives psychologists ways of helping people improve the quality of their lives. Psychologists have devised types of interventions that help people gain control over problematic aspects of their lives. People can harness psychological forces to eliminate unhealthy behaviors like smoking and initiate healthy behaviors like regular exercise. Parenting practices can help parents maintain solid bonds with their children. These are just a few examples of the broad range of circumstances in which psychologists use their knowledge to control and improve people's lives. In this respect, psychologists are a rather optimistic group; many believe that virtually any undesired behavior pattern can be modified by the proper intervention.

—Adapted from Gerrig, and Zimbardo, *Psychology and Life,* 18th ed., p. 8.

9. The best definition of *intervention* is _____.
    a. an action that harms
    b. an action that increases
    c. an action that antagonizes
    d. an action that changes

10. The best definition of *harness* is _____.
    a. utilize
    b. eliminate
    c. connect
    d. destroy

Name_____ Section _____ Date _____ Score (number correct) _____ x 10 = _____

Objective: To locate topics and stated main ideas within paragraphs.

Directions: Read the following paragraph and answer the questions that follow.

[1]Often called the "forgotten nutrient," water is essential to life. [2]Without it, you could live only about one week. [3]About 65 to 70 percent of your body weight is made up of water in the form of blood, saliva, sweat, urine, cellular fluids, and digestive enzymes. [4]In all these various forms, water helps transport nutrients, remove wastes, and regulate body temperature.

— Pruitt & Stein, *Health Styles,* 2nd ed., p. 107

_____1. The topic of the paragraph is _____.
      a. water removes waste
      b. the importance of water
      c. water

_____2. The main idea of the paragraph is expressed in _____.
      a. sentence 1
      b. sentence 2
      c. sentence 3
      d. sentence 4

[1]Fear of skin cancer has given sun exposure a bad rap. [2]However, a healthy body needs short daily doses of sunlight. [3]Direct sunlight helps the body produce vitamin D, and vitamin D helps the body absorb calcium. [4]Sunlight also stimulates the body to produce two important chemicals. [5]One is serotonin, which helps stabilize your moods. [6]The other is melatonin, which helps regulate your sleep cycle.

_____3. The topic of the paragraph is _____.
      a. sunlight
      b. vitamin D
      c. healthy benefits of sunlight

_____4. The main idea of the paragraph is stated in _____.
      a. sentence 1
      b. sentence 2
      c. sentence 3
      d. sentence 5

31

[1]Elizabeth Hobbs Keckley lived from 1818 to 1907. [2]She was born in Virginia, and she learned to read, write, and sew while still a slave. [3]Her skill as a dressmaker to wealthy women in St. Louis enabled her to buy freedom for herself and her son for $1,200 in 1855. [4]By 1860, she had established a dressmaking business in Washington, D.C., that attracted the capital's elite. [5]Her shop boasted a parlor, private fitting room, and upstairs workroom employing a number of seamstresses. [6]When newly elected President Lincoln arrived in the city, his wife inquired where the leading women had their wardrobes made. [7]She was told that they went to Elizabeth Keckley.

— Adapted from New York Historical Society, *Enterprising Women.*

_____5. The topic of the paragraph is _____.
   a. a dressmaking business
   b. Elizabeth Keckley
   c. a successful business woman

_____6. The main idea of this paragraph is expressed in _____.
   a. sentence 1
   b. sentence 2
   c. sentence 3
   d. sentence 5

Directions: Read the following group of ideas and then answer the questions that follow.

(A) Hemingway developed his style as a reporter for the *Kansas City Star*.
(B) Hemingway used short sentences and active, simple language.
(C) American novelist Ernest Hemingway developed a writing style that earned him the Nobel Prize in literature.

_____7. The topic of the group of sentences is _____.
   a. Nobel Prize winners
   b. Ernest Hemingway
   c. Ernest Hemingway's writing style

_____8. Statement (A) is _____.
   a. the main idea
   b. a supporting detail

_____9. Statement (B) is _____.
   a. the main idea
   b. a supporting detail

_____10. Statement (C) is _____.
   a. the main idea
   b. a supporting detail

Name_____ Section _____ Date _____ Score (number correct) _____ x 10 = _____

Objective: To determine topics and main ideas of paragraphs.

Directions: Read the paragraphs and answer the questions that follow.

Paragraph A

[1]When planning a celebration, some people find ways to imbue the event with their personal signature. [2]Brides often seek ways to personalize their wedding receptions, making the event more memorable. [3]For example, they will display a slide presentation of snapshots of the couple's lives from their childhoods through their engagement. [4]Also, they often exhibit photographs of their parents' and grandparents' lives to establish a connection to their pasts as well as a photographic history of both families. [5]Another way to personalize the reception is to have guests engrave their names on a silver platter with an engraving tool or sign the photographic mat that will encompass a portrait of the couple.

1.   The topic of the paragraph is _____.
     a.   celebrations
     b.   personalizing celebrations
     c.   slide presentations
     d.   guest signatures

2.   The main idea of the paragraph is stated in _____.
     a.   sentence 1
     b.   sentence 2
     c.   sentence 3
     d.   sentence 4

Paragraph B

[1]Many businesses are honest, ethical, and honorable. [2]However, some businesses use ploys, or tricks, to attract their patrons. [3]For example, one local furniture store uses the tactic of no down payment, no interest for two years. [4]Another trick used by other businesses includes the offer of free items such as a satellite dish or home security system. [5]While it may look good initially to the consumer, he or she must consider the required monthly and yearly fees, which can compute to exorbitant prices. [6]A third ploy is the attractive display ad with nearly indiscernible fine print. [7]Savvy shoppers learn to scrutinize the content of sale flyers for hidden penalties and misleading or omitted details.

3.   The topic of the paragraph is _____.
     a.   honest business practices
     b.   hidden fees
     c.   deceptive business practices
     d.   deceptive advertising

4.   The main idea of the paragraph is stated in _____.
       a.   sentence 1
       b.   sentence 2
       c.   sentence 3
       d.   sentence 4

Paragraph C

[1]Before you throw away that aluminum can or plastic bottle, think again. [2]Recycling has many advantages that affect all of us. [3]For one, it creates new industries, and it can also lead to the evolution of new products from old ones. [4]Used tires, for instance, often become the material used as ground cover to prevent erosion. [5]Another advantage in recycling is that it reduces the amount of trash transported to landfills, many of which have surpassed their original expected capacity and currently need to be capped.

5.   The topic of the paragraph is _____.
       a.   benefits of landfills
       b.   new uses for old tires
       c.   garbage solutions
       d.   advantages of recycling

6.   The main idea of the paragraph is stated in _____.
       a.   sentence 1
       b.   sentence 2
       c.   sentence 3
       d.   sentence 4

Paragraph D

[1]Although personality psychologists may disagree on the meaning of the word *personality,* most agree that the term originated from the Latin *persona,* that is, the theatrical mask worn by Roman actors in Greek dramas. [2]Despite the original meaning of the word, psychologists now speak of personality as something more than simply the role people play. [3]Personality is a pattern of relatively permanent traits, dispositions, or characteristics that give some consistency to people's behavior. [4]More specifically, personality includes traits or dispositions that lead you to behave at least somewhat consistently in different environmental situations. [5]But the definition of personality must also allow for some inconsistency of behavior. [6]For example, you may behave quite aggressively in one situation but rather submissively in another, depending on the presence of other people, the behavior of those people, and your own mood and motivation.

—Lefton & Brannon, *Psychology,* 8th ed., p. 404.

_____7.   The topic of this paragraph is _____.
       a.   the origin of the word *persona*
       b.   psychology as a science
       c.   personality
       d.   masks worn by Roman and Greek actors

_____8.   The main idea of the paragraph is stated in _____.
       a.   sentence 1
       b.   sentence 2
       c.   sentence 3
       d.   sentence 4

Paragraph D

[1]A classic projective test is the Rorschach Inkblot Test. [2]The test taker sees ten inkblots, one at a time. [3]The blots are symmetrical, with a distinctive form; five are black and white, two also have some red ink, and three have various pastel colors. [4]Examinees tell the clinician what they see in the design, and a detailed report of the response is made for later interpretation.

—Lefton & Brannon, *Psychology*, 8th ed., p. 404.

____9. The topic of this paragraph is _____.
- a. the Rorschach inkblot test
- b. classic psychological tests
- c. the colors of the Rorschach inkblot test
- d. the tools of a psychology clinician

____10. The main idea of the paragraph is stated in _____.
- a. sentence 1
- b. sentence 2
- c. sentence 3
- d. sentence 4

Name_____ Section _____ Date _____ Score (number correct) _____ x 10 = _____

Directions: Read the following passages and answer the questions that follow.

Passage A

1 [1]Throughout its history, the United States has both welcomed immigration and feared its consequences. [2]The gates opened wide (numerically, if not in attitude) for a massive wave of immigrants in the late nineteenth and early twentieth centuries. [3]During the past twenty years, a second great wave of immigration has brought close to a million new residents to the United States each year. [4]Today, more immigrants and children of immigrants (56 million) live in the United States than at any other time in the country's history. [5]Unlike the first wave, which was almost exclusively from western Europe, the second wave is more diverse. [6]In fact, it is changing the U.S. racial-ethnic mix. [7]If current trends in immigration (and birth) persist, in a little over fifty years the "average" American will trace his or her ancestry to Africa, Asia, South America, the Pacific Islands, the Middle East—to almost anywhere but white Europe.

2 [8]As in the past, there is concern that "too many" immigrants will alter the character of the United States. [9]"Throughout the history of American immigration," write sociologists Alejandro Portés and Ruben Rumbaut, "a consistent thread has been the fear that the 'alien element' would somehow undermine the institutions of the country and would lead it down the path of disintegration and decay." [10]A widespread fear in the early 1900s was that immigrants from southern Europe, then arriving in large numbers, would bring communism with them. [11]Today, some fear that Spanish-speaking immigrants threaten the primacy of the English language. [12]In addition, the age-old fear that immigrants will take jobs away from native-born Americans remains strong. [13]Finally, minority groups that struggled for political representation fear that newer groups will gain political power at their expense.

—Henslin, *Essentials of Sociology*, 5th ed., pp. 249–50.

_____1. The topic of the passage is _____.
    a. Americans' conflicting attitudes about immigration.
    b. immigration in the United States.
    c. the first wave of immigration in the United States.
    d. the second wave of immigration in the United States.

_____2. The central idea of the passage is expressed in the thesis statement, which is _____.
    a. sentence 1
    b. sentence 2
    c. sentence 3
    d. sentence 7

_____3. The topic of paragraph 1 is _____.
    a. number of immigrants
    b. problems of immigration
    c. immigration
    d. average Americans

_____ 4. How many waves of immigration are discussed in paragraph 1?
   a. one
   b. two
   c. three
   d. four

_____ 5. The topic of paragraph 2 is _____.
   a. California's changing population
   b. English and Spanish as the main languages of the United States
   c. the effect of immigration on the workforce
   d. fears that some people have about the growing number of immigrants

_____ 6. The main idea of paragraph 2 is expressed in the topic sentence, which states,
   a. As in the past, there is concern that 'too many' immigrants will alter the character of the United States.
   b. A widespread fear in the early 1900s was that immigrants from southern Europe, then arriving in large numbers, would bring communism with them.
   c. Today, some fear that Spanish-speaking immigrants threaten the primacy of the English language.
   d. Finally, minority groups that struggled for political representation fear that newer groups will gain political power at their expense.

Passage B

1 Critical viewing of visual art is difficult at first. Much that is praised in contemporary painting and sculpture may look so unfamiliar that the tendency is to say, "I don't understand it," and drop the subject. Instead, stand back, look carefully at the work, be positive, and try as hard as possible to describe exactly what is there before you: "This is a large canvas, mainly white, with broad strokes of scarlet, resembling comets." The description does not say whether the painting is worth the time to investigate it, but you can never get to evaluating it without first seeing it clearly without a preset attitude.

2 The 1997 blockbuster film *Titanic* offers a good opportunity to practice the skill of noticing. Everyone knows about the disaster that befell the ship and its passengers in 1912. The climax is clear from the beginning. There can be no surprises. What interests us along the way? *Irony*, of course: the opening shots of the magnificent vessel and the champagne bottle confidently broken across the hull; the cheering of the crowd; the proud faces of owners and builders; quick scenes of a few families and couples who will be shown again as the voyage proceeds, people whose lives we know will be ended or changed forever as the ship comes closer and closer to its dread fate; a little further on, quick cuts to the telegraph operators receiving reports of icebergs; and then close-ups of bits of ice floating in the serene waters through which the ship glides, telltale signs that go unnoticed, so that, even though the ending of the film is obvious, the piling up of these details can intensify the emotions of some viewers, even those who may ultimately decide that there is too *much* irony, that the inevitable tragedy is overstated.

—Janaro & Altshuler. *The Art of Being Human*, 7th ed., pp. 25–26.

_____ 7. The topic of the passage is _____.
   a. visual art
   b. critical viewing of visual art
   c. critical viewing of painting
   d. sculpture

_____8. The author's central point about the topic is expressed in which sentence?
  a. Critical viewing of visual art is difficult at first.
  b. Much that is praised in contemporary painting and sculpture may look so unfamiliar that the tendency is to say, "I don't understand it," and drop the subject.
  c. Instead, stand back, look carefully at the work, be positive, and try as hard as possible to describe exactly what is there before you: "This is a large canvas, mainly white, with broad strokes of scarlet, resembling comets."
  d. The description does not say whether the painting is worth the time to investigate it, but you can never get to evaluating it without first seeing it clearly without a preset attitude.

_____9. The topic of paragraph 2 is _____.
  a. irony
  b. irony in film
  c. disaster films
  d. the skill of noticing as applied to irony in *Titanic*

_____10. What is the main idea of paragraph 2?
  a. *Titanic* was a blockbuster film.
  b. Details of irony in *Titanic* provide an opportunity to practice the skill of noticing.
  c. Irony is an excellent visual tool for filmmakers.
  d. The skill of noticing requires practice.

38

Name_____ Section _____ Date _____ Score (number correct) _____ x 10 = _____

Directions: Read the following paragraphs and answer the questions that follow.

[1]Because nicotine is habit-forming, kicking the smoking habit takes time and knowledge. [2]Half of the battle in quitting is knowing you need to quit. [3]This knowledge will help you deal better with the likely symptoms of withdrawal, such as irritability and an intense desire to smoke. [4]A number of quitting methods are available, including nicotine replacement products (gum and patches), but there is no easy way. [5]Nearly all smokers have some feelings of nicotine withdrawal when they try to quit. [6]Give yourself a month to get over these feelings. [7]Take quitting one day at a time, even one minute at a time— whatever you need to succeed.

—Adapted from the National Center for Chronic Disease Prevention and Health Promotion, "Don't Let Another Year Go Up in Smoke."

_____1. The topic of the paragraph is _____.
    a. kicking the smoking habit
    b. the smoking habit
    c. withdrawal symptoms

_____2. The main idea of the paragraph is expressed in _____.
    a. sentence 1
    b. sentence 2
    c. sentence 3
    d. sentence 4

[1]Susan is getting anxious. [2]She is applying to MBA programs and desperately wants to get into a top-ten school. [3]She believes that graduating from a high-ranked business school could make all the difference in recouping the money she will spend getting her MBA. [4]She also knows that admittance to a top program could be difficult. [5]Her friend, an executive recruiter, advises her to "spin" her previous title and experience to make herself look better. [6]Susan isn't sure if this is the right thing to do. Ethical situations like this are a challenge to many young businesspeople.

—Adapted from Wicks, Freeman, Werhane, and Martin, *Business Ethics: A Managerial Approach*, pp.1–2.

_____3. The topic of the paragraph is _____.
    a. Susan's plan for recouping educational expenses
    b. advice for applying to MBA programs
    c. ethical challenges for young businesspeople

_____4. The main idea of the paragraph is stated in _____.
    a. sentence 1
    b. sentence 2
    c. sentence 5
    d. sentence 6

[1]When you think of NASCAR, do you think of tobacco-spitting rednecks in pickup trucks at run-down racetracks? [2]Think again! [3]These days, NASCAR is a great marketing organization that focuses single-mindedly on creating customer relationships. [4]For its fans, NASCAR is a lot more than stock car races. [5]It's a high-octane, totally involving experience. [6]And it is now the second-highest rated regular season sport on TV. [7]Races are seen in 150 countries in 23 languages. [8]There are 75 million NASCAR fans and they are young, affluent, and decidedly family oriented—40 percent are women. [9]A hardcore NASCAR fan spends nearly $700 a year on NASCAR-related clothing, collectibles, ad other items.

—Adapted from Kotler and Armstrong, *Principles of Marketing*, 13th ed., p. 36.

_____5. The topic of the paragraph is _____.
     a. stock car racing
     b. NASCAR's customer relationships
     c. money spent by NASCAR fans

_____6. The main idea of this paragraph is expressed in _____.
     a. sentence 1
     b. sentence 2
     c. sentence 3
     d. sentence 5

Directions: Read the following group of ideas and then answer the questions that follow.

(a) *Law and Order* is a high-quality TV crime drama.
(b) Each week, the show thoughtfully tracks a murder through the police investigation and the trial of the person arrested as responsible for the murder.
(c) The show is entering its 14th season, won an Emmy in 1997 for outstanding drama series, and has been nominated for the award 11 years in a row.

_____7. The topic of the group of sentences is _____.
     a. murder mysteries
     b. award-winning TV dramas
     c. *Law and Order*

_____8. Statement (a) is _____.
     a. the main idea
     b. a supporting detail

_____9. Statement (b) is _____.
     a. the main idea
     b. a supporting detail

_____10. Statement (c) is _____.
     a. the main idea
     b. a supporting detail

Name_____ Section _____ Date _____ Score (number correct) _____ x 10 = _____

Directions: Read the following paragraphs and answer the questions that follow.

Paragraph A

[1]Fatigue can have noticeable short-term effects. [2]First, fatigue affects the body. [3]Long hours of work without rest can result in muscle aches, tension headaches, and eyestrain. [4]Second, fatigue affects the mind. [5]A tired mind turns sluggish, and thoughts can become confused. [6]Third, fatigue affects the emotions. [7]An individual who has worked to the point of exhaustion may become oversensitive and short-tempered. [8]Fourth, not only does fatigue affect the individual, but it also has an immediate effect on the person's work product. [9]A worker who is overtired is more likely to make careless mistakes and turn out a lower-quality product. [10]Finally, exhaustion strains personal relationships by increasing the likelihood of misunderstandings and quarrels.

1.   The topic of the paragraph is _____.
         a.   quarrels
         b.   short-term effects of fatigue
         c.   fatigue
         d.   health problems

2.   The main idea of the paragraph is expressed in _____.
         a.   sentence 1
         b.   sentence 2
         c.   sentence 9
         d.   sentence 10

Paragraph B

[1]By mid-1600, the cost of meeting the Virginia region's need for labor became a major problem. [2]The country resorted to slavery to meet its growing need for labor. [3]The first African blacks brought to English North America arrived on a Dutch ship and were sold at Jamestown in 1619. [4]Early records are vague and incomplete, so it is not possible to say whether these Africans were treated as slaves or freed after a period of years like bond servants. [5]What is certain is that by about 1640, some blacks were slaves (a few, with equal certainty, were free). [6]By the 1660s, local laws had firmly established slavery in Virginia and Maryland.

—Adapted from Garraty & Carnes, *The American Nation,* 10th ed., p. 42.

3.   The topic of the paragraph is _____.
         a.   the beginning of Jamestown
         b.   the beginning of slavery in North America
         c.   slavery
         d.   labor problems in North America

4.   The main idea of the paragraph is expressed in _____.
     a. sentence 2
     b. sentence 3
     c. sentence 4
     d. sentence 6

Paragraph C

[1]The most prominent southern leader in national politics during the early 1800s was William H. Crawford. [2]He served as President Monroe's secretary of the treasury. [3]During his service in the Georgia legislature, he spoke for the large planters against the interest of the small farmers. [4]In 1807, he was elected to the United States Senate. [5]Later he put in a tour of duty as minister to France. [6]Crawford was direct and friendly and a marvelous storyteller, and one of the few persons in Washington who could teach the new senator Martin Van Buren anything about politics. [7]Crawford was one of the first politicians to try to build a national political machine. [8]"Crawford's Act" of 1820, limiting the term of minor federal employees to four years, was passed. [9]As the name of the act suggests, it was passed largely through Crawford's efforts. [10]He realized before nearly anyone else that a handful of petty offices, properly doled out, could win the loyalty of thousands of voters.

—Adapted from Garraty & Carnes, *The American Nation,* 10th ed., p. 215.

5.   The topic of the passage is _____.
     a. southern leaders
     b. first politicians
     c. William H. Crawford
     d. Crawford Acts

6.   The main idea of the paragraph is expressed in _____.
     a. sentence 1
     b. sentence 2
     c. sentence 6
     d. sentence 10

Passage D

1 In January 1964, at age 17, Randy Gardner made history by setting a world's record by staying awake for more than 260 hours—just short of 11 days. He enlisted two friends to help keep him awake, and he took no stimulants, not even coffee. After two days, sleep researcher William Dement began supervising Gardner's progress, much to the relief of his parents. Although Gardner did not suffer any serious physical symptoms, there were marked psychological effects. On day 2, he had trouble focusing his eyes. On day 3, he experienced mood changes. On day 4, he was irritable and uncooperative; he also began to hallucinate. By day 6, Gardner had some memory lapses and difficulty speaking. By day 9, his thoughts and speech were sometimes incoherent. On day 10, blurred vision became more of a problem, and he was regularly forgetting things. Mornings were his most difficult time. Despite these behavioral changes, Randy never became violent or behaved in a socially deviant manner.

2 One of the most interesting aspects of Randy Gardner's adventure is what happened to his sleep after his deprivation. Dement followed up by monitoring and observing Gardner for several days to see how well he recovered, what happened to his sleep patterns, and whether he made up for the sleep he had lost. Dement found that for the three nights following his deprivation, Gardner slept an extra 6.5 hours; on the fourth night, he slept an extra 2.5 hours. Therefore, Randy did not make up the sleep that he lost in his 11 days of sleep deprivation.

3 Randy Gardner's experience was unusual in terms of the length of his sleep deprivation, but going without sleep is a part of many people's lives. According to the National Sleep Foundation, 67% of adults in the United States get less than the recommended amount of sleep; 43% say that sleepiness interferes with activities in their lives, including work performance. People miss sleep in order to work, but they also neglect sleep in order to have fun, such as partying and watching TV. What are the effects of sleep deprivation? How much harm does going without sleep cause, especially at typical levels such as a few hours per night? If Randy Gardner's experience is typical, missing a few hours' sleep doesn't cause many problems, but many hours of deprivation produce major problems in functioning.

—Adapted from Lefton & Brannon, *Psychology,* 8th ed., pp. 197–198.

7.   The topic of the entire passage is _____ .
     a.   sleep
     b.   sleep deprivation
     c.   dreams
     d.   REM sleep

8.   The central point of the passage, expressed in the thesis statement, is:
     a.   Therefore, Randy did not make up all the sleep that he lost in his 11 days of sleep deprivation.
     b.   Randy Gardner's experience was unusual in terms of the length of his sleep deprivation, but going without sleep is a part of many people's lives.
     c.   If Randy Gardner's experience is typical, missing a few hours' sleep doesn't cause many problems, but many hours of deprivation produces major problems in functioning
     d.   The effects of sleep deprivation are actually very mild, and many people could do with less sleep than they currently get.

9.   The topic of paragraph 2 is _____ .
     a.   William Dement, sleep researcher
     b.   Randy Gardner
     c.   the psychological effects of sleep deprivation on Randy Gardner
     d.   sleep patterns after sleep deprivation

10.   Which sentence states the main idea of paragraph 3?
     a.   Randy Gardner's experience was unusual…
     b.   According to the National Sleep Foundation…
     c.   People miss sleep in order to work…
     d.   How much harm does going without sleep cause…

Name_____ Section _____ Date _____ Score (number correct) _____ x 10 = _____

Directions: Read the following paragraphs and answer the questions that follow.

Paragraph A

[1]Budget planning is the process of forecasting future expenses and savings. [2]The first step in budget planning is to evaluate your current financial position by assessing your income, your expenses, your assets (what you own), and your liabilities (debit, or what you owe). [3]Your net worth is the value of what you own minus the value of what you owe. [4]You can measure your wealth by your net worth. [5]As you save money you increase your assets and therefore increase your net worth. [6]Budget planning enables you to build your net worth by setting aside part of your income to either invest in additional assets or reduce your liabilities.

—Adapted from Madura, *Personal Finance,* 3rd ed., p. 4.

1.   The topic of the paragraph is _____.
        a.   assets
        b.   liabilities
        c.   assets and liabilities
        d.   budget planning

2.   The main idea of the paragraph is _____.
        a.   sentence 1
        b.   sentence 2
        c.   sentence 3
        d.   sentence 4

Paragraph B

[1]Advancements in technology often make it possible for us to experience historic events not only moments after they occur, but sometimes even while they occur. [2]For example, images brought to us courtesy of modern technology include the horror of 9/11, the Asian tsunami of 2005, the devastation wrought by hurricane Katrina, and the May 2006 earthquake that killed thousands in Indonesia. [3]We can communicate with people in almost any part of the world; we can send messages via email, fax, and telephone. [4]We can use cameras at our computers or cell phones and visit face to face with people around the globe. [5]We can even turn on the television and see and hear what is happening anywhere in the world or even in space.

—Adapted from Seiler and Beall, *Communication: Making Connections.* 7th ed., p. 10.

3.   The topic of the paragraph is _____.
        a.   devastating events
        b.   mass communication
        c.   advances in communication technology
        d.   digital cameras

44

4.   The main idea of the paragraph is _____.
        a.   sentence 1
        b.   sentence 2
        c.   sentence 4
        d.   sentence 5

Paragraph C

[1]In spite of the many challenges influencing our health, many people have made progress in reducing risks and making healthy lifestyle choices. [2]Developing and maintaining healthy habits by becoming informed consumers takes work, determination, and time. [3]Those who have achieved this goal ask more questions and learn to separate fact from fiction as they negotiate the various paths toward achieving health. [4]In addition, these individuals have identified unique ways to make small changes to sustain long-term, positive behavior change. [5]Consequently, learning to recognize unhealthy behaviors, identifying the factors that influence them, and planning the steps needed to reach personal health goals is a strategy that has worked for many in order to improve health.

—Donatelle, *Access to Health*, 10th ed., p. 4.

5.   The topic of the paragraph is _____.
        a.   becoming informed consumers
        b.   positive behavior change
        c.   healthy lifestyles
        d.   strategies for improving health

6.   The main idea of the paragraph is _____.
        a.   sentences 1 and 5
        b.   sentence 2
        c.   sentence 2
        d.   sentence 4

Passage D

1 [1]A Bureau of Justice study published in 2006 found that local police departments use a variety of applicant-screening methods. [2]Nearly all use personal interviews, and a large majority use basic skills tests, physical agility measurements, medical exams, drug tests, psychological evaluations and background investigations into the personal character of applicants. [3]Among departments serving 25,000 or more residents, about eight in ten use physical agility tests and written aptitude tests. [4]More than half check credit records, and about half use personality inventories and polygraph exams.

2 [5]Effective policing, however, may depend more on innate personal qualities than on educational attainment or credit history. [6]Police administrator August Volmer, one of the first people to attempt to describe the personal attributes necessary in a successful police officer, said that the public expects police officers to have "the wisdom of Solomon, the courage of David, the strength of Samson, the patience of Job, the leadership of Moses, the kindness of the Good Samaritan, the strategic training of Alexander, the faith of Daniel, the diplomacy of Lincoln, the tolerance of the Carpenter of Nazareth, and finally an intimate knowledge of every branch of the natural, biological, and social sciences."

—Adapted from Schmalleger, *Criminal Justice: A Brief Introduction*, 8th ed., p. 228.

45

_____7. The topic of paragraph 1 is _____.
  a. a Bureau of Justice statistics study
  b. police departments
  c. methods to screen police applicants
  d. tests that measure aptitude

_____8. The main idea of paragraph 1 is expressed in _____.
  a. sentence 1
  b. sentence 2
  c. sentence 3
  d. sentence 4

_____9. The topic of paragraph 2 is _____.
  a. police administrator August Volmer
  b. traits of effective police personnel
  c. Biblical references
  d. Educational requirements of police personnel

_____10. The topic of this passage is _____.
  a. screening methods
  b. police personnel
  c. effective personality traits
  d. identifying competent police personnel

Name_____ Section _____ Date _____ Score (number correct) _____ x 10 = _____

Objective: To determine the implied main idea by examining the supporting details.

A. Directions: Choose the best implied main idea for the following groups of supporting details.

A. Supporting details:

- Women who are pregnant should avoid drinking unpasteurized milk.
- Raw or partially cooked eggs, and raw or undercooked meat, fish or poultry may be unsafe for women who are pregnant.
- Expectant mothers should avoid certain soft cheeses such as Brie, feta, and Roquefort cheeses unless these foods are labeled as made with pasteurized milk.
- Pregnant women should avoid certain types of fish because of their high mercury content.

—Adapted from Thompson and Manore, *Nutrition for Life*, 2nd ed., p. 346.

____1. Implied main idea: _____
   a.   People should avoid eating raw seafood.
   b.   Women must be careful of their diets.
   c.   Drinking unpasteurized milk can be dangerous for women who are pregnant.
   d.   A few specific foods may be unsafe for women who are pregnant.

B. Supporting details:

- We have all learned to deal with hard-to-open "childproof" packaging.
- Must drug producers and food makers now put their products in tamper-resistant packages.
- In making packaging decisions, the company must heed growing environmental concerns.
- Most companies have gone "green" by reducing their packaging and using environmentally responsible packaging materials.

—Adapted from Kotler and Armstrong, *Principles of Marketing*, 13th ed., p.232.

____2. Implied main idea: _____
   a.   Children must be kept safe from both prescription and non-prescription medicines.
   b.   Safety and environmental concerns are now major packaging issues for companies.
   c.   Packaging has gone to ridiculous lengths in order to keep children safe.
   d.   Environmental concerns are an important issue for manufacturing companies.

B. Directions: Read the following paragraphs, then choose the best statement of the implied main idea for each paragraph.

Women have now become a majority of the students on college campuses across the United States. As their numbers have increased, women have become well represented in many fields of study that once excluded them, including mathematics, chemistry, and biology. But men still predominate in many fields, including engineering, physics, and philosophy. Women choose fields more in the visual and performing arts, English, foreign languages, and the social sciences. More men than women take computer science, and courses in gender studies enroll mostly women.

—Adapted from Macionis, *Sociology*, 13th ed., p. 333.

_____ 3.   Which sentence best states the implied main idea?
    a.   Gender continues to shape career choices on college campuses.
    b.   More women than men are attending college.
    c.   Women are now taking college courses that were traditionally once denied to them.
    d.   Although more women are enrolling in college than men, they continue to be treated unfairly.

Lewis and Clark gathered a group of 48 experienced men near St. Louis during the winter of 1803-1804. In the spring, they made their way slowly up the Missouri River in a 55-foot keelboat and two dugout canoes, called pirogues. By late fall, they had reached what is now North Dakota, where they built a small station, Fort Mandan, and spent the winter. In April 1805, having shipped back to President Jackson more than 30 boxes of plants, minerals, animal skins and bones, and Indian artifacts, they struck out again toward the mountains. They were accompanied by a Shoshone woman, Sacajawea, and her husband, who acted as guides. They passed the Great Falls of the Missouri. They clambered over the Continental Divide at Lemhi Pass in southwest Montana. They descended from the Rocky Mountains to the Pacific by way of the Clearwater and Columbia Rivers. By 1806, the group had concluded its explorations of the Louisiana Purchase and returned to St. Louis.

—Adapted from Garraty & Carnes, *The American Nation,* 10th ed., p. 180.

_____ 4.   Which sentence best states the implied main idea?
    a.   Lewis and Clark spent too many months exploring the United States.
    b.   From 1803 to 1806, Lewis and Clark led the exploration of the Louisiana Purchase.
    c.   The United States was uncharted territory until the Lewis and Clark exploration.
    d.   Lewis and Clark needed the help of guides in order to make their way over very mountainous terrain.

When Stephanie was an infant, she frequently became ill and spent a lot of her infancy in the doctor's office. Antibiotics were delivered by injections. The shots were obviously painful and caused Stephanie to scream and cry. Of course, the doctor in his white coat and the nurse in her white uniform were always present, as well as the white paper covering the examining table. It didn't take too many visits before Stephanie would scream when she saw the "white coat" people coming toward her.

—Adapted from Ciccarelli and White, *Psychology*, 2nd ed., p. 176.

48

_____5.   Which sentence best states the implied main idea?
     a.   Stephanie hated injections.
     b.   Doctors and nurses should not wear white.
     c.   Stephanie spent an unusual amount of time in the doctor's office when she was a baby.
     d.   Stephanie learned to associate white coats and being up on a table with pain.

A credit card class refers to the credit level of the cardholder. At the low end is the standard with credit limits from $500 to $3,000. Above that are Gold cards such as the Visa Gold card, which offer a bigger line of credit, generally $5,000, and up, and provide extra perks or incentives. Finally, there are premium or prestige credit cards, such as the MasterCard Platinum card, which offer credit limits as high as $100,000 or more and benefits beyond a standard credit card, such as emergency medical and legal services, travel insurance and services, rebates, and warranties on new purchases. Now, Visa and MasterCard even offer Titanium cards, with higher credit limits and even more benefits.

—Adapted from Keown, *Personal Finance: Turning Money into Wealth*, 5th ed., p. 171.

_____6.   Which sentence best states the implied main idea?
     a.   Reward programs are a gimmick that entice people to accept credit cards they don't need.
     b.   There are several different classes of credit cards.
     c.   Credit cards should be used for emergency situations only.
     d.   Consumers should choose a credit card with the highest limits possible in order to take advantage of all the perks that come with the card.

In the United States, we say that housework is important to family life. Here, as around the world, taking care of the home and children has always been considered "women's work." As women have entered the labor force, the amount of housework women do has gone down, but the share done by women has stayed the same. Overall, women average 16.1 hours a week of housework, compared to 10.5 hours for men.
—Adapted from Macionis, *Sociology*, 13th ed., p. 337.

_____7.   Which sentence best states the implied main idea?
     a.   While men may support the idea of women entering the labor force, most husbands resist taking on a more equal share of household duties.
     b.   Most men believe that women should stay home and take care of the family and household duties.
     c.   Men would probably do more housework if their spouses gave them more praise.
     d.   Doing housework and taking care of families is the responsibility of the wife because everyone knows that women are more nurturing and do a better job at this kind of work.

On March 23, 2007, hotel Heiress Paris Hilton attended a birthday party for namesake celebrity gossip blogger Perez Hilton in West Hollywood, California. This was only two months after pleading no contest to an alcohol-related reckless driving offense in Los Angeles. Hilton was sentenced to three years' probation, fined $1500 plus court costs, and ordered to participate in an alcohol-education program. Stopped for driving with her lights out not long afterward, she was then ordered to spend time in jail—a sentence that was completed in June 2007.

—Adapted from Schmalleger, *Criminal Justice: A Brief Introduction*, 8th ed., p. 362.

49

_____8. Which sentence best states the implied main idea?
- a. Paris Hilton is extremely wealthy.
- b. Paris Hilton was afraid to go to jail.
- c. Celebrities should not be subject to the same laws and fines as everyone else.
- d. The punishment for Paris Hilton's driving offenses was minimal and did very little to teach her to obey the laws.

C. Directions: Read the following paragraph and answer the questions that follow.

The *Wall Street Journal*, the staunch advocate of capitalism, has called Karl Marx (1818-1883) one of the three greatest modern thinkers (the other two being Sigmund Freud and Albert Einstein). Marx, who came to England after being exiled from his native Germany for proposing revolution, believed that the engine of human history is **class conflict**. He said that the *bourgeoisie* (the controlling class of *capitalists,* those who own the means to produce wealth—capital, land, factories, and machines) are locked in conflict with the *proletariat* (the exploited class, the mass of workers who do not own the means of production). This bitter struggle can end only when members of the working class unite in revolution and throw off their chains of bondage. The result will be a classless society, one free of exploitation, in which people will work according to their abilities and receive according to their needs.

—Adapted from Henslin, *Essentials of Sociology*, 5th ed., p. 5.

_____9. The topic of the passage is _____.
- a. Wall Street's three greatest modern thinkers
- b. Karl Marx
- c. Karl Marx and class conflict theory
- d. capitalism

_____10. Which sentence best states the implied main idea of the paragraph?
- a. Karl Marx is one of the most intelligent men who have ever lived.
- b. Karl Marx was a revolutionary leader.
- c. Karl Marx and his theory of class conflict had a great influence on world history.
- d. Karl Marx was considered a dangerous man in Germany because of his ideas.

Name_____ Section _____ Date _____ Score (number correct) _____ x 10 = _____

Objective: To determine the implied main ideas and central idea.

A. Directions: Read each group of supporting details. Then, choose the best implied main idea for each group.

A. Supporting details:

- In 2000, the average woman having her first baby was almost 25 years old.
- The average age of mothers rose from 24.6 years to 27.2 over three decades.
- The number of women in the labor force has gone up by almost 40 percent.
- Women may also delay having children due to changes in birth control, social support, and marriage patterns.

—National Center for Health Statistics,
"American Women Are Waiting to Begin Families."

_____1. Implied main idea: _____
   a. Most American women are 25 years old when they have their first baby.
   b. Women are delaying having children for several reasons.
   c. By the year 2000, fewer American women were having children.
   d. More women are entering the work force than at any time in American history.

B. Directions: Read the following paragraphs; then choose the best statement of the implied main idea for each paragraph.

_____2. Yao Ming is 7 feet 5 inches tall and weighs nearly 300 pounds. He plays professional basketball for the Houston Rockets. Among National Basketball Association rookies in the 2003 season, Yao ranked second in scoring average, second in rebounding average, first in blocks per game, and third in field goal percentage. In 2003, Yao Ming also took an active part in the battle against SARS; he hosted a live telethon in his homeland, China, to raise money to research its cure.
   a. Yao Ming is an unusually large basketball player.
   b. Yao Ming is an unusual basketball player for many reasons.
   c. Yao Ming used his fame to fight disease.
   d. Yao Ming plays basketball for the Houston Rockets.

_____3. Be careful about the kind of information you put in an e-mail or on a Web site; both are public forms of communication. Be aware that you are not anonymous; every piece of information that you send through the Web or e-mail can be traced to you. Be brief and clear in your subject headings and messages. Be considerate of others; don't forward chain letters, and use respectful language.
   a. Many people engage in rude behavior when communicating on the Internet.
   b. Communicating on the Internet or through e-mail is risky.
   c. Internet users should follow a few basic guidelines to ensure safety and courtesy.
   d. It is important to be brief and clear when communicating on the Internet.

51

_____4. The last three miles had been the hardest. By now the first 23 miles seemed like a foggy dream brought on by fatigue. During the last hour, she had debated with every running step about just quitting. Every step, she debated and kept on running. And now the sight of the finish line brought a new surge of emotion. She called on all her will and strength and picked up her pace. Weary, sore, with head held high, Yesenia finished her first marathon in just under five hours—long after the strong runners had cooled down.
   a. Yesenia was tempted to drop out of the marathon.
   b. Yesenia is a talented marathon runner who placed well in the race.
   c. Yesenia's first marathon ended in pain and frustration.
   d. Yesenia finished her grueling first marathon with the attitude of a winner.

_____5. People can experience positive outcomes and personal growth from deeply negative events. People may also experience posttraumatic growth (positive psychological change) in response to serious illnesses, accidents, natural disasters, and other traumatic events.
   —Adapted from Gerrig, and Zimbardo, *Psychology and Life,* 18th ed., p 402.

   a. People should avoid negative stress events at all costs.
   b. Posttraumatic growth is an odd response to traumatic events.
   c. Personal growth is an important aspect of maturity.
   d. Negative events can lead to positive outcomes.

_____6. Masculine organizations emphasize competitiveness and aggressiveness. They focus on the bottom line and reward their workers on the basis of their contribution to the organization. Feminine organizations are less competitive and less aggressive. They're more likely to emphasize worker satisfaction and reward their workers on the basis of need.
   —Adapted from DeVito, *The Interpersonal Communication Book*, 11th ed. p. 42.

   a. Masculine organizations are more successful than feminine organizations.
   b. Most men would not want to work for a feminine organization.
   c. Feminine organizations should learn how to be more competitive.
   d. Organizations can be viewed in terms of masculinity or femininity.

_____7. Because infants are so small, they proportionally lose more water through evaporation than do adults. Also, their kidneys are immature and unable to concentrate urine. Hence, they are at increased risk of dehydration. An infant needs about 2 fl oz of fluid per pound of body weight. Experts recently confirmed that "infants exclusively fed human milk do not require supplemental water." The practice common among some low-income families of diluting infant formula with extra water is extremely dangerous. Overhydration can cause nutrient imbalances such as hyponatremia (low blood sodium) as well as inadequate weight gain and failure to thrive.

   — Adapted from Thompson and Manore, *Nutrition for Life*, 2nd ed.,

   a. Fluid is critical for everyone.
   b. Infants have immature kidneys that cannot adequately process fluids.
   c. The balance of fluids in infants is critical for two reasons.
   d. Low-income families often cannot afford expensive infant formula.

C. Directions. Read the following passage from a college communications textbook. Identify the central idea in the space provided.

Evaluating consists of judging the messages you hear. At times, you may try to evaluate the speaker's underlying intent. Often you evaluate without being aware that you are doing so. For example, Elaine tells you she is up for a promotion and is really excited about it. You may then try to judge her intention. Does she want you to use your influence with the company president? Is she looking for a pat on the back? Generally, if you know the person well, you will be able to identify the intention and respond properly.

In other situations, your evaluation is more in the nature of critical thinking. For example, in a business meeting on upgrading office equipment, you would evaluate the request as you are listening to it. You would ask yourself, "Are the requests logical? Will they increase output? What is the evidence? Are there better solutions?" In order to answer these questions, you first should resist evaluating until you fully understand the speaker's point of view. Second, assume that the speaker is a person of good will, and ask the speaker to explain any unclear points. Third, separate facts from personal opinions. Finally, identify any biases or self-interests that may lead the speaker to slant the facts.

—Adapted from DeVito, Essentials of Human Communication, 4th ed., p. 83.

_____ 8. Which sentence best states the implied main idea of the first paragraph?
    a. We don't always judge a speaker's intent correctly unless we know him or her well.
    b. Speakers often have hidden intentions which they try to hide.
    c. Most speakers are actually looking for a pat on the back.
    d. We are always suspicious of underlying intentions while listening to others.

_____ 9. Which sentence best states the implied main idea of the second paragraph?
    a. You must be on your guard during business meetings.
    b. Critical thinking requires no special skills.
    c. Business meetings require unique forms of communication.
    d. Business people use critical thinking skills while listening.

_____ 10. What is the implied central idea of the passage?
    a. Listeners often misjudge a speaker's intentions.
    b. Listeners can use several techniques to evaluate a speaker more effectively.
    c. Speakers who are familiar are far easier to understand.
    d. Speakers are often biased and may slant the facts in their own interest.

Name_____ Section _____ Date _____ Score (number correct) _____ x 10 = _____

A. Directions: Read each group of supporting details. Then, choose the best implied main idea for each group.

A. Supporting details:

- Create a quiet, private environment.
- Sit at eye level with the client.
- Demonstrate interest with the client's concerns.
- Maintain confidentiality.

—Adapted from Kozier and Erb, *Fundamentals of Nursing: Concepts, Process, and Practice,* 8th ed., p. 1008.

____1. Implied main idea: _____
   a. A nurse can follow several steps to establish trust and a working relationship.
   b. Creating client trust is very difficult.
   c. It is impossible to establish a good relationship without trust.
   d. Clients concerns should be of the utmost importance.

B. Directions: Choose the best implied main idea of each paragraph.

____2. When you click onto the site rockthevote.org, you get this message: "Rock the Vote is dedicated to protecting freedom of expression and to helping young people realize and utilize their power to effect change in the civic and political lives of their communities." Rock the Vote is a blend of new politics and new media. It began in 1990 to fight censorship in the recording industry, but it quickly grew to become a campaign to register voters.

—Adapted from Folkerts & Lacy, *The Media in Your Life: An Introduction to Mass Communication,* 2nd ed., p. 3.

   a. Rock the Vote is a Web site dedicated to young people.
   b. Rock the Vote protects freedom of expression.
   c. Rock the Vote has evolved into a political and civic Web site for young people.
   d. Rock the Vote originally was formed to fight censorship.

____3. The potential for anonymity on the Internet cloaks many criminals in legitimate-looking identities, allowing them to place fraudulent orders with online merchants. They can also steal information by intercepting e-mail or shut down e-commerce sites by using software viruses. The Internet was never designed to become a global marketplace with a billion users.

—Adapted from Laudon and Traver, *E-commerce,* 3rd ed., p. 248.

   a. There are many legitimate businesses and online sites on the Internet.
   b. The Internet has become a global commercial entity.
   c. The Internet wasn't designed with security features that prevent fraudulent activity.
   d. Spreading computer viruses should be considered a major crime.

_____4. Police departments often become problem identifiers in communities. The police have learned that if vacant buildings are left untended, if graffiti is tolerated, and if public order violations such as public drinking, disruptive behavior by youths, and vandalism are permitted, these will be signals to people that nobody cares about the community. This is known as the broken window syndrome.

—Aadapted from Fagin, *Criminal Justice,* 2nd ed., p. 295.

    a. A community with the broken window syndrome will be more vulnerable to serious crime.
    b. Most policemen prefer to work with community problems rather than other areas of law enforcement.
    c. A broken window sends the message that people can't afford repairs.
    d. Police have more tolerance for problems in communities than for people who break the law.

_____5. Athletes and others use a technique known as imagined rehearsal to reach their goals. By visualizing their planned action ahead of time, they will be prepared when they put themselves to the test. For example, suppose you want to ask someone out on a date. Imagine walking together to class. Then practice in your mind and out loud exactly what you're going to say. Mentally anticipate different responses and what you will say in reaction.

—Donatelle, *Access to Health*, 10th ed., p. 29.

    a. Extensive preparation is necessary before asking someone out on a date.
    b. Most people are not success the first time they ask someone on a date.
    c. Careful mental and verbal rehearsal will greatly improve the likelihood of success.
    d. Athletes are better at reaching their goals than most people because of their training.

_____6. On average, women retire earlier than men, largely because family events—a husband's retirement or the need to care for an ill spouse or parent—play larger roles in their decisions. Women in or near poverty, however, are an exception. Lacking financial resources to retire, many continue working into old age. This trend is especially pronounced among women of some ethnic groups, who are more likely to have minimal retirement benefits and to be caring for other family members.

—Adapted from Berk, *Development Through the Lifespan,* 4th ed., p. 626.

    a. Retirement decisions vary with gender and ethnicity.
    b. For many, eligibility for retirement benefits may be postponed to a later age.
    c. Health factors affect retirement decisions.
    d. Women are more financially able to retire earlier than men.

_____7. Biologists have so far identified and named about 1.8 million species, the term used for a particular type of organism, such as *Pelecanus occidentalis*, the brown pelican. Researchers identify thousands of additional species each year. Estimates of the total number of species range from 10 million to over 200 million. How do we make sense of this much diversity?

—Campbell, Reece, Taylor, and Simon, *Biology: Concepts & Connections*, 5th ed., p. 6.

    a. Finding names for all of the new species is a constant challenge for scientists.
    b. Diversity is a characteristic of life.
    c. No one scientist could count all of the species on the earth.
    d. Biologists are the scientists who identify and name new species of life.

_____8. According to Carol Kleiman, columnist for the *Chicago Tribune* newspaper, many firms screen out candidates over the phone who do not demonstrate minimal levels of enthusiasm or communication skills. She cites David Stiefel, consultant with PeopleScout, a Chicago-based firm, who says that about 65 percent of all job candidates are screened out for those reasons. He goes on to suggest that you can successfully obtain an on-site interview on the phone by speaking in a clear, concise voice and by sounding enthusiastic about the job.

—Adapted from Seiler and Beall, *Communication: Making Connections*. 7th ed., p. 481.

    a. Job applicants should hire a consultant in order to get through the interview process successfully.
    b. Job applicants must be prepared to handle phone interviews successfully.
    c. Most businesses now do all of their job interviewing by telephone.
    d. Most businesses hire consultants to handle the initial screening process of job applicants.

_____9. Indirect messages allow you to express a desire without insulting or offending anyone. They also allow you to observe the rules of polite interaction. So instead of saying, "I'm bored with this group," you say, "It's getting late and I have to get up early tomorrow," or you look at your watch and pretend to be surprised by the time. In each instance, you're stating a preference but are saying it indirectly so as to avoid offending someone. Sometimes indirect messages allow you to ask for compliments in a socially acceptable manner, such as saying, "I was thinking of getting my eyes done." You hope to get the desired compliment: "Your eyes? They're perfect as they are."

—Adapted from DeVito, *The Interpersonal Communication Book*, 11th ed. p. 130.

    a. Polite interaction often requires delicate handling.
    b. People often insult one another without realizing it.
    c. Indirect messages are often hypocritical—saying one thing but meaning another.
    d. Indirect messages have several advantages.

____10. If you are far from retirement, you might consider investing your retirement contributions in mutual funds that invest in stocks with high potential for growth. This might be a capital appreciation fund, a technology fund, or maybe an international stock or bond fund. If you are close to retirement, you might consider Ginnie Mae bond funds, Treasury bond funds, or a stock mutual fund that pays high dividends. If you are young and far from retirement, you are in a position to take more risk with your investments. As you approach retirement, however, your investments should be more conservative.

—Adapted from Madura, *Personal Finance,* 3rd ed., pp. 560–561.

    a. Your retirement plan decisions should take into account the number of years until you retire.

    b. Stocks are usually considered more high risk than mutual funds.

    c. People near retirement should look for investments that will pay high dividends.

    d. Young people who are far from retirement can allow for more risk in their investment decisions.

57

Name_____ Section _____ Date _____ Score (number correct) _____ x 10 = _____

A. Directions: Choose the best implied main idea for the following groups of supporting details.

A. Supporting details:

- A thin, brittle, low-density layer of rock called the *crust* covers Earth's surface and rests atop a thick layer of denser rock called the *mantle*.
- The mantle surrounds a dense core consisting mostly of iron, solid in the inner core and molten in the outer core.
- A portion of the upper mantle called the *asthenosphere* contains especially soft rock, melted in some areas.
- The harder rock above the *asthenosphere* is what we know as the *lithosphere*, and this includes both the crust and the upper mantle.

> —Adapted from Withgott and Brennan, *Essential Environment: The Science Behind the Stories*, 3rd ed., p. 235.

_____1. Implied main idea: _____
   a. The planet Earth is composed of many layers of solid rock.
   b. The planet Earth has an unstable core that is molten.
   c. The planet Earth consists of multiple layers.
   d. The earth's crust is very thin and brittle.

B. Supporting details:

- Usually, verbal and nonverbal behaviors reinforce or support each other.
- For example, you don't usually express fear with words while the rest of your body relaxes.
- You don't normally express anger with your body posture while your face smiles.
- Your entire being works as a whole to express your thoughts and feelings.

> —Adapted from DeVito, *The Interpersonal Communication Book*, 12th ed., p.99.

_____2. Implied main idea: _____
   a. Both verbal and nonverbal signals occur simultaneously to express emotion.
   b. Verbal communication is the primary way we express ourselves.
   c. Fear and anger are normally expressed through nonverbal communication.
   d. Smiling is an example of nonverbal communication.

B. Directions: Read the following paragraphs; then choose the best statement of the implied main idea for each paragraph.

Simple tasks such as making hotel reservations would be nearly impossible without a credit card. Credit cards can be used as identification when cashing checks, for video rental memberships, and almost anywhere else multiple pieces of identification are needed. And using credit extends your shopping opportunities—it's nearly impossible to make a purchase over the phone or the Internet without a credit card. You will receive an itemized billing of exactly how much you spent and where you spent it when

58

shopping with a credit card. In addition, you also reduce the risk of theft associated with carrying around large amounts of cash. Finally, open credit is a source of temporary emergency funds. So, credit frees you to put your money in higher-yielding investments because you don't need to keep as much in liquid emergency funds.

—Adapted from Keown, *Personal Finance: Turning Money into Wealth*, 5th ed., p. 169.

_____3. Which sentence best states the implied main idea?
    a. Credit cards are an excellent source of identification.
    b. Credit cards must be kept safe because they can easily be stolen.
    c. Using credit cards will enable you to become a better investor.
    d. There are several good reasons for using a credit card in today's society.

Each year, in early March, more than 350, 000 Harley bikers rumble through the streets of Daytona Beach, Florida, to attend the Daytona Bike Week celebration. Bikers from across the nation lounge on their low-slung Harleys, swap biker tales, and sport T-shirts proclaiming, "I'd rather push a Harley than drive a Honda." "You don't see people tattooing Yamaha on their bodies," observes the publisher of *American Iron*, an industry publication. And according to another industry insider, "For a lot of people, it's not that they want a motorcycle; it's that they want a Harley."

—Adapted from Kotler and Armstrong, *Principles of Marketing*, 13th ed., p. 134.

_____4. Which sentence best states the implied main idea?
    a. Motorcycle riders have more tattoos than most other people.
    b. The Daytona Bike Week celebration is overrun by Harley fans.
    c. Harley owners are intensely loyal to the Harley-Davidson brand.
    d. Harley Davidson motorcycles are a better bike than Yamahas or Hondas.

During the past 20 years, there has been phenomenal growth in the restaurant industry, particularly the fast-food market. During this same period, rates of obesity have increased dramatically. The portion sizes of packaged foods and restaurant meals have expanded considerably over the past 40 years. For example, the energy provided in a McDonald's lunch is enough to support an entire day's needs for a small sedentary woman. Recent studies indicate that when children and adults are presented with large portions of foods and beverages, they eat more overall and often fail to realize when they are full.

—Adapted from Thompson and Manore, *Nutrition for Life*, 2nd ed., p.271 & 276.

_____5. Which sentence best states the implied main idea?
    a. People who eat fast-food meals will become obese.
    b. Understanding what a healthful portion size is has become a challenging issue today.
    c. McDonald's lunches are not healthy for a normal-sized person.
    d. Obesity problems exist because of fast-food restaurants.

John F. Kennedy's death made Lyndon B. Johnson president. From 1949 until his election as vice-president, Johnson had been a senator and, for most of that time, Senate Democratic leader. He could be heavy-handed or subtle and also devious, domineering, persistent, and obliging. Many people swore by him; few had the fortitude to swear at him. Above all, he knew what to do with political power. "Some men," he said, "want power so they can strut around to 'Hail to the Chief'. . . . I wanted to use it."

Johnson, who had consciously modeled his career after that of Franklin D. Roosevelt, considered social welfare legislation his specialty. The contrast with Kennedy could not have been sharper. In his inaugural address, Kennedy had made no mention of domestic issues. Kennedy's plans for federal aid for education, urban renewal, a higher minimum wage, and medical care for the aged were blocked in Congress by Republicans and southern Democrats. The same coalition also defeated his chief economic initiative—a broad tax cut to stimulate the economy. But Kennedy had reacted to these defeats mildly, almost wistfully. He thought the machinery of the federal government was cumbersome and ineffective.

Johnson knew how to make it work. On becoming president, he pushed hard for Kennedy's programs. Early in his career Johnson had voted against a bill making lynching a federal crime, and he also had opposed bills outlawing state poll taxes and establishing the federal Fair Employment Practices Commission. But after he became an important figure in national affairs, he consistently championed racial equality. Now he made it the centerpiece of his domestic policy. "Civil righters are going to have to wear sneakers to keep up with me," he boasted. Bills long buried in committee sailed through Congress. Early in 1964 Kennedy's tax cut was passed. A few months later, an expanded version of another Kennedy proposal became law as the Civil Rights Act of 1964.

—Carnes & Garraty, *The American Nation,* 11th ed., pp. 798–799.

_____ 6. The topic of the passage is _____.
   a. Kennedy's influence on civil rights
   b. Johnson's presidency and its effect on social reform
   c. Johnson's early career in opposition to social reform
   d. the effect of Kennedy's death on the country

_____ 7. Which sentence best states the implied main idea of the first paragraph?
   a. Lyndon B. Johnson succeeded as president after John F. Kennedy's death.
   b. Lyndon B. Johnson had been in government many years before becoming president.
   c. Lyndon B. Johnson both desired and understood how to use political power when he became president after the death of John F. Kennedy.
   d. Lyndon B. Johnson had many undesirable personality traits.

_____ 8. Which sentence best states the implied main idea of the second paragraph?
   a. President Kennedy was an ineffective leader of the United States.
   b. President Kennedy did not get along well with Congress.
   c. President Kennedy felt that the government of the United States was managed poorly.
   d. President Lyndon B. Johnson led the country in a very different way from the leadership style of President John F. Kennedy.

60

_____9. Which sentence best states the implied main idea of the third paragraph?
   a. President Lyndon B. Johnson successfully implemented many programs initiated by former President John F. Kennedy.
   b. Unlike former President John F. Kennedy, President Lyndon B. Johnson supported the civil rights movement.
   c. President Lyndon B. Johnson did not support federal tax cuts.
   d. Lynching was legal in the United States before President Lyndon B. Johnson outlawed it.

_____10. Which sentence best expresses the central idea of the passage?
   a. Johnson's presidency, modeled after that of Franklin Roosevelt, successfully championed many social reform issues.
   b. Kennedy was concerned about civil rights but ineffective in changing government policies.
   c. Kennedy's death was the reason civil rights reforms were effectively initiated.
   d. Johnson was a strong man, impossible to oppose and used to getting his own way.

Name_____ Section _____ Date _____ Score (number correct) _____ x 10 = _____

A. Directions: Read each group of supporting details. Then, choose the best implied main idea for each group.

Supporting details:

- In 2004, over 25 percent of all arrests were attributed to drug abuse.
- Since 1992, the number of inmates incarcerated for drug-related offenses has risen from approximately 430,000 to 660,000.
- Drug abuse is also a societal and health problem.
- In 2002, the estimated societal cost of drug abuse attributable to health-care costs was more than 180 billion.

—Adapted from Laudon and Traver, *E-commerce,* 3rd ed., p. 139.

_____1. Implied main idea: _____
   a. Crimes involving drug abuse have risen over the past decade.
   b. In addition to begin a serious criminal justice problem, drug abuse is a societal and health problem.
   c. Society should realize that it is impossible to stop drug abuse.
   d. Too much money is being wasted on people who abuse drugs.

B. Directions: Read each of the following paragraphs and choose the implied main idea.

_____2. Hail usually forms when a cold front passes during a thunderstorm. Some experts believe that hailstones gather size as they fall straight down. Others believe that hail is formed and blown about in tall clouds. As hailstones move about in the clouds, they gather size until they are too heavy to be sustained by the wind and fall to the ground.
   a. Scientists fully understand the nature of hailstones.
   b. Experts disagree about the formation and behavior of hailstones.
   c. Experts agree that thunderstorms always produce hailstones.
   d. Much of our weather phenomena is unexplainable.

_____3. Fetal alcohol syndrome (FAS) is one of the three most common causes of birth defects. These birth defects may include mental retardation, damage to the nervous system, and damage to major organs. In addition, these babies are born underweight and grow more slowly than healthy infants. FAS babies have small heads with flat faces and sunken nose bridges. FAS can be prevented by avoiding alcohol consumption during pregnancy.
   a. The serious birth defects and health problems of FAS can be prevented.
   b. Babies born with fetal alcohol syndrome often suffer from mental retardation.
   c. Only babies suffer from FAS.
   d. Healthy infants don't experience the problems of babies born with FAS.

____4. Howard Gardner's work with multiple intelligences has influenced many researchers and educators. For example, Gardner recognized that a person with linguistic intelligence likes to learn by reading and writing stories. Another type of intelligence Gardner identified was spatial; this person learns by drawing, building, and imagining things. In all, Gardner identified eight types of intelligence.
   a. Howard Garner is the leading expert on multiple intelligence.
   b. Linguistic intelligence is just one type of intelligence identified by Howard Gardner
   c. Howard Gardner's identification of eight types of intelligence has influenced researchers and educators.
   d. Researchers and educators depend on the work of Howard Garner in order to make difficult educational decisions.

____5. Children develop language skills through recognizable and documented stages. Most children between the ages of two and three become word-conscious. They need to attach a name to everything in sight that appears. At this stage, children like to repeat sentences and phrases they hear in their surroundings, even if they have no idea of their meaning or if they become annoying. Children simply like the sound and the taste of words.

—Adapted from Janaro and Altshuler, *The Art of Being Human,* 8th ed., p.

   a. Repetition is an important part of the process of acquiring language.
   b. Children between the ages of two and three can be extremely annoying.
   c. Children are born with an instinctive need to acquire language.
   d. Language is a universal trait.

____6. Unlike many other policies, both health care and the environment involve life-and-death decisions. Second, both health policy and environmental decisions involve sophisticated technologies that are expensive and sometimes controversial. Many of these issues involve moral debates as well. Finally, prices for energy, as well as health care, have soared.

—Adapted from Edwards, Wattenberg, and Lineberry, *Government in America: People, Politics, and Policy,* 13th ed., 589.

   a. Health-care policies and environmental policies share many common traits.
   b. There are many difficult issues that must be resolved in our health-care policies.
   c. Environmental policies include decisions that involve great sums of money.
   d. Health care and the environment are two of the greatest concerns for this country.

____7. Multifamily group therapy (MFGT) aims to improve family functioning by bringing together two or more families of parents with their children to meet with a professional therapist. Families receiving MFGT were compared against a randomly assigned group of families receiving traditional family therapy. The study reported that although both groups improved, the MFGT group attended social services for a longer period of time, had fewer dropouts, and received more services when compared to the traditional family therapy group.

—Adapted from Allen-Meares and Fraser, *Intervention with Children and Adolescents: An Interdisciplinary Perspective,* pp. 142–143.

   a. Multifamily group therapy is a promising approach for helping dysfunctional families.
   b. Dysfunctional families require extensive therapy in order to show improvement.
   c. Any type of therapy, no matter which kind, will help families improve.
   d. Traditional family therapy needs to be re-evaluated for its effectiveness.

63

C. Directions. Read the following passage and answer the questions that follow.

A stereotype is a relatively fixed mental picture of some group that is applied to each individual of the group without regard to his or her unique qualities. It's important to note that although stereotypes are usually thought of as negative, they may also be positive. You can, for example, consider certain groups lazy or criminal, but you can also consider them honest or hardworking.

Regardless of whether such stereotypes are positive or negative, however, the problems they create are the same. They provide shortcuts that are usually wrong. For example, when you see someone through a stereotype, you fail to devote enough attention to his or her unique traits. There is nothing wrong with classifying. In fact, it's an extremely useful method of dealing with any complex matter; it puts order into thinking. The problem arises not from classification itself but from applying a label to a class and using that label as the rule for each and every individual in the group.

    —Adapted from Seiler and Beall, *Communication: Making Connections,* 7th ed., p. 401.

_____8.   Which sentence best states the implied main idea of the first paragraph?
     a.   Groups of people can be described according to their stereotypical image.
     b.   People often fail to ignore the individuals who are part of a large group.
     c.   Stereotypes are useful for identifying positive qualities.
     d.   Stereotypes are positive or negative images that are sometimes inappropriately applied to individuals

_____9.   Which sentence best states the implied main idea of the second paragraph?
     a.   Stereotypes are a problem in that they are often wrong.
     b.   Classifying is just as useful a method as stereotyping.
     c.   Putting labels on a group is helpful in describing the individuals of that group.
     d.   Classifying is often helpful, but it should not be used as a rule for all individuals.

_____10. Which sentence best states the implied central idea?
     a.   Although classifying is a useful method of thinking, stereotyping often limits thinking.
     b.   A stereotype can be either negative or positive.
     c.   Stereotyping is one form of classifying, which is a helpful method of thinking.
     d.   Stereotyping ignores an individual's special or unique qualities.

Name _____ Section _____ Date _____ Score (number correct) _____ x 10 = _____

Directions: Read each group of supporting details. Then, choose the best implied main idea for each group.

Supporting details:
- Amazon.com is a business-to-consumer site that sells consumer products to retail consumers.
- ChemConnect.com is a business-to-business exchange site that creates an electronic market for chemical producers and users.
- eBay.com is a consumer-to-consumer site that creates a market space where consumers can auction or sell goods directly to other consumers.
- Gnutella is a peer-to-peer software application that permits consumers to share music with one another directly, without intervention.

—Adapted from Fagin, *Criminal Justice,* 2nd ed., p. 641.

____1. Implied main idea: _____
   a. Business-to-consumer is the most common type of e-commerce.
   b. Online markets have become very popular with consumers.
   c. There are a variety of different types of e-commerce sites.
   d. E-commerce has brought some fundamental changes in the way we do business.

____2. Consider a word such as "death." To a doctor, this word might mean the point at which the heart stops beating. This is denotative meaning, a rather objective description of an event. To a mother whose son has just died, however, the word means much more. It recalls the son's youth, his ambitions, his family, his illness, and so on. To her, the word is emotional, subjective, and highly personal. These emotional, subjective, and personal associations are the word's connotative meanings.

—Adapted from DeVito, *The Interpersonal Communication Book*, 11th ed. p. 130.

   a. Words can have both denotative and connotative meanings.
   b. Denotative meanings are more objective and impersonal.
   c. Connotative meanings are subjective and highly personal.
   d. Death has many different meanings for different people.

____3. Bombing of buildings (such as the attacks on New York and Washington on September 11, 2001, on the American embassy in Kenya in 1998; and on the World Trade Center in New York in 1993) is just one form of terrorism. Terrorism has also included bombing of ships (the USS COLE in Yemen in 2000), the assassinations of political leaders (as when Iraq attempted to kill former president George Bush in 1993), and the kidnappings of diplomats and civilians (as when Iranians took American hostages in 1979).

—Adapted from Edwards, Wattenberg, and Lineberry, *Government in America: People, Politics, and Policy,* 13th ed., p. 631.

   a. It is difficult to defend against terrorism, especially in an open society.
   b. Terrorists have the advantage of stealth and surprise.
   c. Terrorism can never be stopped.
   d. Terrorism takes many forms.

65

_____4.   4.   As you write checks, you should record them in your checkbook so that you can always determine how much money is in your account. By keeping track of your account balance, you can make sure that you stay within your limit when writing checks. This is very important because you are charged fees when you write a check that bounces. In addition, you might lose some credibility when writing bad checks, even if it is unintentional.

—Adapted from Madura, *Personal Finance,* 3rd ed., p. 125.

    a.   Checking accounts allow you to draw on funds by writing checks against your account.
    b.   Most people keep a checking account so that they do not have to carry much cash.
    c.   You should monitor your checking account balance frequently.
    d.   Writing bad checks is can get you in trouble.

_____5.   5.   Addictive exercisers abuse exercise in the same way that alcoholics abuse alcohol or addictive spenders abuse money. They use it compulsively to try to meet needs—for nurturance, intimacy, self-esteem, and self-competency—that aren't being met in more acceptable ways. As a result, addictive exercise results in negative consequences similar to those found in other addictions: alienation of family and friends, injuries from overdoing it, and a craving for more.

—Adapted from Donatelle, *Access to Health*, 10th ed., p. 363.

    a.   Exercise can be addictive.
    b.   Many people develop unhealthy exercise patterns.
    c.   Addictions are basically all the same.
    d.   Addictive exercisers often suffer from social problems.

_____6.   6.   Life originated in the sea and evolved there for almost three billion years before plants and animals began moving onto land. As you just learned in Module 34.6, their evaporation provides most of Earth's rainfall, and ocean temperatures have a major effect on climate and wind patterns. Photosynthesis by marine algae and cyanobacteria supplies a substantial portion of the earth's oxygen.

—Campbell, Reece, Taylor, and Simon, *Biology:*
Concepts & Connections, 5th ed., p. 690.

    a.   We would not have air to breathe if it were not for our oceans.
    b.   Oceans have had and continue to have an enormous impact on Earth.
    c.   Much of the earth is covered by oceans.
    d.   Ocean temperatures play a large role in the earth's climate and weather.

_____7.   7.   Betrayal can happen when someone trusts another person and, in one way or another, that trust is broken. For example, if you tell a friend a personal secret and especially ask for complete confidentiality and the friend then spreads the story to others, you have been betrayed. Relationships that are injured by deception and betrayal are often not repairable because of the amount of hurt such breaches of trust cause.

—Adapted from Seiler and Beall, *Communication: Making Connections*. 7th ed., p. 394.

    a.   People should realize the consequences before trusting friends with secrets.
    b.   Secrets are best kept to yourself.
    c.   Betrayal is a warning sign that a relationship is in trouble.
    d.   Friends should never reveal secrets about friends.

8.   Corporal punishment is often carried out in public so that others may witness the event. For example, in the Iranian flogging for drinking alcohol, over 1,000 people gathered in Vali-e-Asr Square in Teheran to watch the lashings. In England and the United States, hangings were once a public event, and parents brought their children to witness what happens when one breaks the law. Some advocates

66

of general deterrence today propose that the death penalty would be a greater deterrent to crime if executions were broadcast live on television.

—Aadapted from Fagin, *Criminal Justice,* 2nd ed., p. 440.

 a. Punishments in foreign countries are far more inhumane than in the United States.
 b. Some believe that witnessing pain suffered by those who commit crimes will be a deterrent to future crimes.
 c. The death penalty has proven to be a successful deterrent to crime.
 d. Executions will be broadcast soon on television.

9. Estimates of the prevalence of mood disorders reveal that about 21 percent of females suffer a major depression at some time in their lives compared to 13 percent of males. One factor that contributes to this difference is that on average, women experience more negative events and life stressors than men do. For example, women have a greater likelihood of experiencing physical or sexual abuse, and they are more likely to live in poverty while being the primary caregiver for children and elderly parents.

—Adapted from Gerrig, and Zimbardo, *Psychology and Life,* 18th ed., p. 467.

 a. Women are more prone genetically to experience depression than men.
 b. Caring for elderly parents and children leads to depression.
 c. Both men and women experience negative events and life stressors.
 d. Women suffer from depression almost twice as often as men.

10. In 1990, a 26-year-old Terri Schiavo's heart stopped briefly, temporarily cutting off oxygen to her brain. She lay in a persistent vegetative state as a result. Her husband and guardian, Michael, claimed that she had earlier told him she would not want to be kept alive artificially, but Terri's parents disagreed, and a long court case ensued. The decision to keep her alive or to remove her feeding tube bounced back and forth between the courts. Finally, 15 years later, Terri Schiavo died after her feeding tube was removed for a third time.

—Adapted from Berk, *Development Through the Lifespan,* 4th ed., p. 650.

 a. No one should have the right to withhold treatment, permitting a patient to die.
 b. Making end-of-life decisions can involve heated controversy when the patient's wishes are unclear.
 c. The courts should never have interfered in the Terri Schiavo case.
 d. Feeding tubes should not be allowed when there is no hope for recovery.

Name_____ Section _____ Date _____ Score (number correct) _____ x 10 = _____

Objective: To identify the topic, main idea, major, and minor supporting details in a passage.

Directions: Read the following passage and answer the questions that follow.

[1]Victims and witnesses of gang violence face additional and serious problems. [2]One problem is that victims and witnesses usually live with or among the persons responsible for of the crime. [3]A second problem is that victims and witnesses often face an entire gang, as opposed to a sole attacker. [4]The gang members to blame for the violence are even likely to attend the funeral of the victim. [5]As a result, victims and witnesses are often frightened and so do not cooperate with the criminal justice system. [6]They are fearful of retaliation if they do. [7]A third major problem is that victims and survivors are often seen as contributors to the crime. [8]This is particularly true for surviving family members of murdered children, some of whom were members of gangs. [9]The belief of "contribution" leads some victim compensation programs to deny funds to victims and survivors of gang violence. [10]Victim blaming is considerable, with frequent questions being asked, for instance, "Why didn't you just move away from your gang-infested neighborhood?" or "Why was your child out, and why don't you control that child?" [11]In addition, victims are frequently afraid or unable to exercise victims' rights. [12]Because of threats, fear of retaliation, or due to poverty or culture, many victims of gang violence do not exercise their rights. [13]Another difficulty some victims face is that they are indigent and cannot afford transportation to court to exercise their right to be present. [14]Moreover some gang violence victims do not speak English and do not understand their rights or the offender's status because this information is conveyed only in English. [15]Finally, some victims simply don't trust the government.

—Adapted from "Victims of Gang Violence: A New Frontier in Victim Services." *Victims of Gang Violence Planning Group. Department of Justice.* 25 Oct. 1996.

_____1. The topic of this passage is _____.
   a. the increase in gang violence
   b. victim blaming and contribution
   c. problems faced by victims and witnesses to gang violence
   d. fears of victims and witnesses to gang violence

_____2. Which sentence is the topic sentence that states the topic and the author's controlling point about the topic?
   a. sentence 1
   b. sentence 2
   c. sentence 3
   d. sentence 11

_____3. Sentence 2 serves as a _____ for the paragraph.
   a. controlling statement
   b. main idea statement
   c. major supporting detail
   d. minor supporting detail

_____ 4. Sentence 7 serves as a _____ for the paragraph.
    a. controlling statement
    b. main idea statement
    c. major supporting detail
    d. minor supporting detail

_____ 5. Sentence 8 serves as a _____ for the paragraph.
    a. controlling statement
    b. main idea statement
    c. major supporting detail
    d. minor supporting detail

_____ 6. Sentence 9 serves as a _____ for the paragraph.
    a. controlling statement
    b. main idea statement
    c. major supporting detail
    d. minor supporting detail

_____ 7. The last major detail is stated in _____.
    a. sentence 12
    b. sentence 13
    c. sentence 14
    d. sentence 15

_____ 8. Which of the following words or phrases in the passage indicates a list of major details?
    a. one, second, in addition, finally
    b. as a result
    c. this is particularly true
    d. because of

_____ 9. According to the context clues and the information in sentence 13, the word _indigent_ means
_____.
    a. uneducated
    b. poor
    c. not from the United States
    d. frightened

_____ 10. According to the passage, why do compensation programs sometimes deny funds to victims and survivors of gang violence?
    a. many don't trust the government and are afraid to ask for help
    b. many don't speak English and can't understand the requirements
    c. they are often seen as contributors to the crime
    d. they don't know how to exercise their rights

Name_____ Section_____ Date_____ Score (number correct) _____ x 10 = _____

Objective: To identify the topic, main idea, and supporting major and minor details in a textbook passage.

Directions: Read the following passage from a sociology textbook, and answer the questions that follow.

[1]Gender inequality is not some accidental, hit-or-miss affair. [2]Rather, the institutions of each society work together to maintain the group's particular forms of inequality. [3]Customs, often venerated through our history, both justify and maintain these arrangements. [4]In the United States, gender inequality is evident in education, health care, and the workplace.

Gender Inequality in Education. [5]Gender inequality in education is not readily apparent. [6]More women than men go to college, and they earn 56 percent of all bachelor's degrees and 57 percent of all master's degrees. [7]A closer look, however, reveals gender tracking, which is a critical problem that reinforces male-female distinctions. [8]Here are two extremes: Men earn 83 percent of bachelor's degrees in the "masculine" field of engineering, while women are awarded 88 percent of bachelor's degrees in the "feminine" field of library "science." [9]Because socialization gives men and women different orientations to life, they enter college with gender-linked aspirations. [10]It is their socialization—not some presumed innate characteristics—that channels men and women into different educational paths.

—Adapted from Henslin, *Essentials of Sociology,* 5th ed. pp. 264–265.

_____1. The topic of the passage is
    a. gender tracking
    b. women in education
    c. women in the United States
    d. gender inequality in the United States

_____2. The thesis statement of the passage is expressed in _____.
    a. sentence 1
    b. sentence 2
    c. sentence 3
    d. sentence 4

_____3. The topic of the second paragraph is _____.
    a. gender tracking in education
    b. feminine fields of study
    c. masculine fields of study
    d. socialization

_____4. The main idea of the second paragraph is expressed in _____.
    a. sentence 5
    b. sentence 6
    c. sentence 7
    d. sentence 8

70

_____5. According to the section "Gender Inequality in Education," what percentage of women earn master's degrees?
   a. 56 percent
   b. 57 percent
   c. 65 percent
   d. 75 percent

_____6. The term *gender tracking* refers to _____.
   a. ways in which women are studied by sociologists for statistical purposes
   b. ways in which men are studied by sociologists for statistical purposes
   c. ways in which women are encouraged by feminists to break through barriers
   d. ways in which men are encouraged to seek degrees in "masculine" fields and women are reinforced to pursue "feminine" fields

_____7. Sentence 8 serves as a _____ for the paragraph.
   a. main idea
   b. supporting detail
   c. thesis statement
   d. summary statement

_____8. Sentence 10 serves as a _____ for the paragraph.
   a. main idea
   b. major supporting detail
   c. minor supporting detail
   d. summary statement

_____9. According to the paragraph, women enter more "feminine" fields of study because _____.
   a. these are more suitable professions for women
   b. they are discouraged to enter "masculine" fields by their colleges
   c. they can't afford the higher costs associated with other professions
   d. of their socialization

_____10. According to this passage, library science is considered a more _____ field.
   a. feminine
   b. masculine
   c. neutral
   d. difficult

71

Name_____ Section_____ Date_____ Score (number correct) _____ x 10 = _____

Directions: Read the following passage, and then answer the questions that follow.

[1]The general success of Asian Americans can be traced to three major factors: family life, educational achievement, and assimilation into mainstream culture.

[2]Of all ethnic groups, including whites, Asian American children are the most likely to grow up in a stable family. [3]They usually have two parents and are least likely to be born to a single mother. [4]Most grow up in close-knit families that stress self-discipline, thrift, and hard work. [5]This early socialization provides a strong impetus for the other two factors.

[6]The second factor is their high rate of college graduation. [7]Forty-two percent of Asian Americans complete college. [8]To realize how stunning this is, compare the statistics: 26% for white Americans, 11% for Latinos, 15% for African Americans, and 11% for Native Americans. [9]The educational achievement of Asian Americans opens doors to economic success.

[10]Assimilation, the third factor, is indicated by several measures. [11]With about two of five marrying someone of another racial-ethnic group, Asian Americans have the highest intermarriage rate of any group. [12]They also are the most likely to live in integrated neighborhoods. [13]Japanese Americans, the financially most successful Asian Americans, are the most assimilated. [14]About 73% say that their best friend is not a Japanese American.

—Adapted from Henslin, *Essentials of Sociology,* 5th ed., pp. 242, 246–247.

_____1. The topic of this passage is _____.
    a. the growing number of Asian Americans in the world
    b. the number of successful Japanese Americans in the United States
    c. the reasons behind the success of Asian Americans
    d. the percentage of Asian Americans with college degrees as compared to other ethnic groups

_____2. The central idea of the passage is stated in _____.
    a. sentence 1
    b. sentence 2
    c. sentence 5
    d. sentence 13

_____3. The main idea of the second paragraph is stated in _____.
    a. sentence 2
    b. sentence 3
    c. sentence 4
    d. sentence 5

_____4. How many major details support the central idea of this passage?
- a. 2
- b. 3
- c. 5
- d. 7

_____5. Which words in the passage serve as clues to the major details?
- a. _general success_ and _assimilation_
- b. _of all groups_ and _most_
- c. _three major factors_
- d. _several measures_

_____6. Sentence 4 serves as a _____ for the entire passage.
- a. topic
- b. main idea
- c. major detail
- d. minor detail

_____7. Sentence 6 serves as a _____for the entire passage.
- a. topic
- b. central idea
- c. major detail
- d. minor detail

_____8. The last major detail is stated in _____.
- a. sentence 10
- b. sentence 11
- c. sentence 12
- d. sentence 14

_____9. According to the context clues and the information in the passage, _assimilation_ is closely related to _____.
- a. integration
- b. socialization
- c. graduation
- d. education

_____10. Which ethnic group has the lowest rate of college graduation?

- a. Latinos
- b. African Americans
- c. Native Americans
- d. white Americans

73

Name_____ Section _____ Date _____ Score (number correct) _____ x 10 = _____

Directions: Read the paragraphs and answer the questions that follow.

[1]In 1996, Pan American Health Organization, an office of the World Health Organization (1996), became concerned about the rise of tuberculosis (TB) around the world. [2]Tuberculousis was then named as the world's deadliest infection due to its devastating traits and rapidly increasing incidents of the disease. [3]TB kills 3 million people (including 300,000 children) each year. [4]TB currently kills more adults each year than AIDS, malaria, and tropical diseases combined.

[5]Approximately one-third of the world's population is infected by the tuberculosis bacterium (*Mycobacterium tuberculosis*). [6]Someone in the world is newly infected with TB literally with every tick of the clock, one person per second. [7]Left untreated, one person with active TB will infect 10 to 15 people in a year's time. [8]At this rate, it is estimated that, in the next decade, 300 million more people will become infected, that 90 million people will develop the disease, and 30 million people will die from it.

[9]The infectious bacteria that causes TB lodges in the lungs and can, in time, spread to the rest of the body. [10]The TB bacilli invade and inflame the respiratory system. [11]As a result, fibrous and hardened materials encase the bacilli. [12]These encased bacilli are called *tubercles*. [13]The TB is arrested at this point, not cured. [14]This period of arrest is known as *primary tuberculosis*.

[15]When the immune system is weakened, the bacilli become active again and *secondary tuberculosis* occurs. [16]Then, extensive lesions and cavities occur in the upper portion of the lungs. [17]Over time, the following symptoms may develop: persistent coughing, weight loss, fever, night sweats, and spitting up blood (Purtilo, 1978). [18]Persons whose immune systems have been weakened by AIDS, diabetes mellitus, malnutrition, or alcoholism are more open to TB.

[19]TB is spread through the air and by casual contact. [20]When infectious people sneeze, cough, or talk, the TB bacilli in their lungs are expelled into the air where they can remain suspended for hours. [21]Then, the TB bacilli can be inhaled by others (WHO, 1996). [22]However, only 5-10 percent of people who are infected with TB actually become sick or infectious themselves, because the immune system "walls off" the TB organisms (WHO, 1996).

[23]Two major factors have contributed to the rise of TB in the United States. [24]First, the accelerated spread of human immunodeficiency virus (HIV), which leads to AIDS, increases the possibility of TB infecting the patient because of his or her weakened immune system. [25]TB and HIV form a deadly combination, each having an effect on the other. [26]The second factor is the number of new immigrants and refugees entering the United States. [27]The largest number of foreign-born people with TB originated from Mexico, the Philippines, Haiti, India, the People's Republic of China, and Vietnam. [28]In 1993, about one- fourth of reported tuberculosis cases were in people who were born outside of the United States.

—Adapted from Nakamura, Raymond A. *Health in America, a Multicultural Perspective.*
Allyn & Bacon, 1999. pp. 220–21.

74

____1. The topic of this passage is _____.
   a. the rise of deadly diseases
   b. the rise and traits of tuberculosis
   c. challenges caused by the spread of deadly diseases
   d. the number of people who have succumbed to tuberculosis

____2. Sentence 1 is a _____.
   a. controlling statement
   b. main idea statement
   c. major supporting detail
   d. minor supporting detail

____3. Sentence 2 serves as a _____ for the paragraph.
   a. controlling statement
   b. contrasting statement
   c. major supporting detail
   d. minor supporting detail

____4. Sentence 7 serves as a _____ for the paragraph.
   a. controlling statement
   b. main idea statement
   c. major supporting detail
   d. minor supporting detail

____5. Sentence 8 serves as a _____ for the paragraph.
   a. controlling statement
   b. main idea statement
   c. major supporting detail
   d. minor supporting detail

____6. Sentence 9 serves as a _____ for the paragraph.
   a. controlling statement
   b. main idea statement
   c. major supporting detail
   d. minor supporting detail

____7. Sentence 23 serves as _____ for the paragraph.
   a. controlling statement
   b. main idea statement
   c. major supporting detail
   d. minor supporting detail

____8. Sentence 24 serves as _____ for the paragraph.
   a. controlling statement
   b. main idea statement
   c. major supporting detail
   d. minor supporting detail

____9. Which of the following words or phrases in the last paragraph indicates the major details?
   a. two major factors
   b. which leads to
   c. *having an effect*
   d. first and second

____10. According to the context clues and the information in sentences 11 and 12, *encase* means _____.
   a. surround
   b. break up
   c. destroy
   d. make up

Name_____ Section _____ Date _____ Score (number correct) _____ x 10 = _____

Directions: Read the paragraph, and answer the questions.

[1]Despite your best efforts to manage the flow of your personal information or to keep it to yourself, skilled identity thieves may still gain access to your data. [2]For your protection, you must be aware of the following ways impostors can get your personal information and take over your identity. [3]They steal wallets and purses containing your identification and credit and bank cards. [4]They steal your mail, including your bank and credit card statements, pre-approved credit offers, new checks, and tax information. [5]They complete a "change of address form" to divert your mail to another location. [6]They rummage through your trash, or the trash of businesses, for personal data in a practice known as "dumpster diving." [7]They fraudulently obtain your credit report by posing as a landlord, employer, or someone else who may have a legitimate need for, and legal right to, the information. [8]They find personal information in your home. [9]They use personal information you share on the Internet. [10]They scam you, often through email, by posing as legitimate companies or government agencies you do business with. [11]Finally, they get your information from the workplace in a practice known as "business record theft" through several methods. [12]They steal files out of offices where you're a customer, employee, patient, or student; they bribe an employee who has access to your files; or they "hack" into electronic files.

—Adapted from "ID Theft: When Bad Things Happen to Your Good Name."
Federal Trade Commission. Nov. 2003.

_____1. The topic of this paragraph is _____.
     a. theft
     b. identity theft
     c. email scams
     d. how identity theft occurs

_____2. Which sentence is the topic sentence that states the topic and the author's controlling point about the topic?
     a. sentence 1
     b. sentence 2
     c. sentence 3
     d. sentence 12

_____3. Sentence 4 serves as a _____for the paragraph.
     a. main idea
     b. major supporting detail
     c. minor supporting detail
     d. central idea

_____4. Sentence 5 serves as a _____ for the paragraph.
        a. main idea
        b. major supporting detail
        c. minor supporting detail
        d. topic

_____5. Sentence 11 serves as a _____ for the paragraph.
        a. main idea
        b. major supporting detail
        c. minor supporting detail
        d. summarizing sentence

_____6. Sentence 12 serves as a _____ for the paragraph.
        a. main idea
        b. major supporting detail
        c. minor supporting detail
        d. concluding sentence

_____7. How many major supporting details are in this paragraph?
        a. 1
        b. 2
        c. 3
        d. 4 or more

_____8. Which word or phrase in sentence 11 signals that minor details will follow?
        a. *finally*
        b. *information*
        c. *business record theft*
        d. *through several methods*

_____9. According to the paragraph *dumpster diving* involves _____.
        a. obtaining credit card reports in dumpsters
        b. diverting mail to another location, usually near a dumpster
        c. rummaging through trash cans for personal data
        d. sifting through information at landfills, looking for prescriptions

_____10. *Business record theft* can occur through all of the following *except* _____.
        a. reading a construction estimate
        b. stealing files out of offices
        c. bribing employees who have access to files
        d. hacking into electronic files

Name_____Section _____ Date _____Score (number correct) _____ x 10 = _____

Directions: Read the paragraph, and answer the questions that follow.

[1]Most of these issues of science and society also involve technology. [2]Science and technology are interdependent, but their basic goals differ. [3]The goal of science is to understand natural phenomena. [4]In contrast, the goal of technology is generally to apply scientific knowledge for some specific purpose.

[5]The potent combination of science and technology has dramatic effects on society. [6]For example, discovery of the structure of DNA by James D. Watson and Francis Crick some 50 years ago and subsequent achievements in DNA science have led to the many technologies of DNA engineering that are transforming many fields including medicine, agriculture, and forensics (DNA fingerprinting, for example).

[7]Technology has improved our standard of living in many ways, but not without consequences. [8]Technology that keeps people healthier has enabled the Earth's population to grow more than tenfold in the past three centuries, to double to over six billion in just the past 40 years. [9]The environmental effects of this growth can be devastating. [10]Global warming, toxic wastes, acid rain, deforestation, nuclear accidents, and extinction of species are just some of the repercussions of more and more people wielding more and more technology.

[11]Science can help us identify such problems and provide insight into which course of action may prevent further damage. [12]But solutions to these problems have as much to do with politics, and economic and cultural values as with science and technology. [13]Now that science and technology have become such powerful aspects of society, every thoughtful citizen has a responsibility to develop a reasonable amount of scientific literacy.

—Campbell, Reece, Taylor, and Simon,
Biology: Concepts & Connections, 5th ed., p. 12.

_____1. The topic of this passage is _____.
   a. science
   b. technology
   c. environmental effects of technology
   d. the aspects of science and technology

_____2. The controlling idea of the passage is expressed in _____.
   a. sentence 1
   b. sentence 5
   c. sentence 8
   d. sentence 11

_____3. Which sentence states the main idea in the first paragraph?
     a. sentence 1
     b. sentence 2
     c. sentence 3
     d. sentence 4

_____4. The words *for example* in sentence 6 indicate that this sentence serves as a _____ for the paragraph.
     a. topic
     b. main idea
     c. supporting detail
     d. central idea

_____5. Sentence 8 serves as a _____ for the second paragraph.
     a. major supporting detail
     b. minor supporting detail
     c. main idea sentence
     d. topic

_____6. The main idea of paragraph 3 is expressed in _____.
     a. sentence 8
     b. sentence 9
     c. sentence 10
     d. sentence 11

_____7. Sentence 10 serves as a _____ for the third paragraph.
     a. topic
     b. main idea
     c. major supporting detail
     d. minor supporting detail

_____8. According to the article, some of the benefits of technology and science include all of the following *except* _____.
     a. advances in DNA engineering
     b. advances in medicine
     c. advances in forensics
     d. limiting the world population

_____9. Some of the harmful effects of technology and science include all of the following *except* _____.
     a. global warming
     b. preserving species
     c. toxic wastes
     d. deforestation

_____10. This article suggests that the responsibility for solving the problems concerning science and technology rests with _____.
     a. every citizen
     b. the government
     c. the field of science
     d. the field of technology

Name_____ Section _____ Date _____ Score (number correct) _____ x 10 = _____

Objective: To outline major and minor details that support the central idea.

Directions: Read the paragraphs and answer the questions that follow.

[1]For as long as nations and international trade have existed, people have debated whether a country is better off with free international trade or with protection from foreign competition. [2]Opponents to free trade pose three main arguments to support their view. [3]The first is the national security argument. [4]They argue that free trade endangers national security and that a country must protect industries that produce defense equipment and armaments as well as those on which the defense industries rely for their raw materials.

[5]The second case for protection and restriction of international trade is the infant-industry argument. [6]This is based on the idea of learning-by-doing. [7]Opponents to free trade contend that the new industry must be protected to enable it to grow into a mature industry capable of competing in a world market. [8]Learning-by-doing is a powerful engine of productivity growth, and comparative advantage evolves and changes because of on-the-job experience.

[9]The third argument for protection against free trade is dumping, which occurs when a foreign firm sells its exports at a lower price than its cost of production. [10]A firm that wants to gain a global monopoly might use dumping. [11]In this case, the foreign firm takes advantage of its monopoly position and charges a higher price for its product.

_____ 1. The central idea of the passage is stated in _____.
     a. sentence 1
     b. sentence 2
     c. sentence 3
     d. sentence 4

_____ 2. The central idea is supported by _____.
     a. characteristics of free trade
     b. a list of arguments opposing free trade
     c. examples of free trade
     d. comparisons between practices that support and oppose free trade

_____ 3. Sentence 3 serves as _____.
     a. the topic of the entire passage
     b. the central idea of the entire passage
     c. a major detail supporting the central idea
     d. a minor detail supporting the first major point

_____ 4. Sentence 5 serves as a _____.
     a. the central idea of the passage
     b. the main idea of the second paragraph
     c. a major detail supporting the second paragraph
     d. a minor detail supporting the second paragraph

81

____5. The third major supporting detail for the central idea is stated in _____.
    a. sentence 2
    b. sentence 8
    c. sentence 9
    d. sentence 11

____6. The phrase that introduces the main idea of the third paragraph is _____.
    a. *the third argument*
    b. *this occurs*
    c. *a firm that*
    d. *in this case*

____7. Which of the following sentences serves as a minor detail supporting a major point?
    a. sentence 1
    b. sentence 2
    c. sentence 4
    d. sentence 5

8–10. Fill in the outline by completing the heading and filling in the two major details that are missing.

Arguments against _____

1. _____

2. _____

3. the dumping argument

82

CHAPTER 6: OUTLINES AND CONCEPT MAPS
Lab 6.2 Practice Exercise 2

Name_____ Section _____ Date _____ Score (number correct) _____ x 10 = _____

Objective: To map the major and minor details supporting a central idea.

Directions: Fill in the concept map with supporting details from the passage.

Passage A

Cultural factors affect our food choices and eating patterns in several ways. First of all, the customs of many cultures put food at the center of celebrations of festivals and holidays, and overeating is encouraged. A second factor is that both parents now work outside the home in most American families. Consequently, more people are now embracing the "fast-food" culture, preferring and almost exclusively choosing highly processed and highly caloric fast foods from restaurants and grocery stores. Finally, coinciding with these cultural influences on food intake are cultural factors that promote an inactive life. Research with sedentary ethnic minority women in the United States indicates that there are some common barriers to a more active lifestyle. These include lack of personal motivation, lack of role models who are physically active, acceptance of larger body size, the viewpoint that exercise is culturally unacceptable, and fear for personal safety.

—Adapted from Thompson and Manore, *Nutrition for Life*, 2nd ed., p. 268.

_____1. The best heading for a concept map of this paragraph is _____.
- a. Factors of Culture
- b. Cultural Factors
- c. Cultural Factors That Affect Eating and Weight Gain
- d. Barriers to an Active Lifestyle

_____2. The major details in this paragraph are intended to _____.
- a. explain the influences of ethnic cultures
- b. list the three factors that influence food choice and eating behavior
- c. describe the problems of the fast-food industry
- d. analyze the barriers to self-motivation

83

3-5. Insert the details that support the central idea in the concept map below.

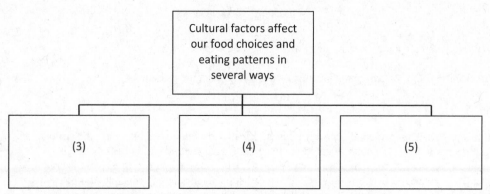

Passage B: Several Types of Microorganisms Contaminate Foods

[1]Two types of food-borne illness are common: *food infections* result from the consumption of food containing living microorganisms, whereas *food intoxications* result from consuming food in which microorganisms have secreted poisonous substances called *toxins*. [2]The microorganisms that most commonly cause food infections are bacteria and viruses.

[3]According the CDC, the majority of food infections are caused by **bacteria**. [4]Of the several species involved, *Campylobacter jejuni* is one of the most common culprits. [5] *Salmonella* is also a leading bacterial culprit in food infections. [6]Raw and undercooked eggs, poultry, meat, and seafood are commonly infected.

[7]The microorganisms just discussed cause illness by directly infecting and destroying body cells. [8]In contrast, some bacteria and fungi cause illness indirectly, by secreting chemicals called toxins into foods. [9]One of the most common and deadly toxins is produced by the botulism toxin. [10]Common sources of contamination are split or pierced bulging cans, food improperly canned at home and raw honey. [11]Some fungi produce poisonous chemicals called *mycotoxins*. [12]These toxins are typically found in grains, peanuts, and other crops stored in moist environments. [13]A highly visible fungus that causes food intoxication is the poisonous mushroom. [14]Most mushrooms are not toxic, but a few, such as the "death cap" mushroom, can be fatal.

—Adapted from Thompson and Manore, *Nutrition for Life*, 2nd ed., pp. 386, 388–389.

_____ 6. Sentence 5 serves as a _____.
     a. main idea for paragraph 2
     b. major detail supporting the main idea for paragraph 2
     c. minor detail supporting a major detail for paragraph 2
     d. central idea of the passage

_____7. Sentence 6 serves as a _____.
    a. main idea for paragraph 2
    b. major detail supporting the main idea for paragraph 2
    c. minor detail supporting a major detail for paragraph 2
    d. conclusion for the paragraph

8-10. Complete the concept map by filling in the blanks.

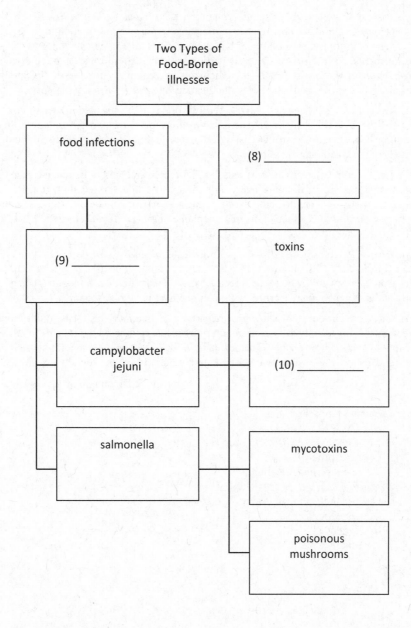

Name_____ Section _____ Date _____ Score (number correct) _____ x 10 = _____

Objective: To outline major and minor details that support the central idea.

Directions: Read the paragraphs and answer the questions that follow.

[1]Are you a fan of *The Weakest Link,* or do you prefer *Who Wants to Be a Millionaire?* [2]These two television shows are similar—both require participants to retrieve information that they have stored in memory. [3]They differ in rules and format, but a major difference is the way that each asks participants to access information. [4]*The Weakest Link* asks participants to recall information by reproducing it, whereas *Who Wants to Be a Millionaire?* requires participants to recognize information. [5]Psychologists use these two measures of retention, plus another method called *relearning,* to study memory.

Recall. [6]In recall tasks participants have to retrieve previously presented information. [7]Not only *The Weakest Link* but also fill-in-the-blank and essay exams require recall of information. [8]In experiments, the information usually comprises strings (lists) of digits or letters. [9]A typical study might ask participants to remember and recall ten items in a list.

[10]Three widely used recall tasks are free recall, serial recall, and paired-associate tasks. [11]In *free-recall tasks,* participants are to recall items in any order, much as you might recall the items on a grocery list. [12]*Serial-recall tasks* are more difficult; the items must be recalled in the order in which they were presented, as you would recall the digits in a telephone number. [13]In *paired-associate tasks,* participants are given a cue to help them recall the second item of a pair of items.

Recognition. [14]In a multiple-choice test, as in *Who Wants to Be a Millionaire?*, you are asked to recognize information. [15]Psychologists have found that recognition tasks help them measure subtle differences in memory ability better than recall tasks. [16]That's because although a person may be unable to recall details of a previously learned fact, he or she may recognize them.

Relearning. [17]No current game show uses relearning as a memory task—it wouldn't make a very exciting show. [18]This technique assesses memory by measuring how long it takes to relearn material that a participant has learned previously. [19]The rationale for this assessment is that rapid relearning indicates some residual memory, and you can quickly relearn material because you already have some memory.

—Lefton & Brannon, *Psychology,* 8th ed. pp. 278–279.

_____1. The topic of this passage is
     a. *The Weakest Link*
     b. *Who Wants to Be a Millionaire?*
     c. recognition
     d. retention and relearning

_____2. The central idea of the passage is stated in _____.
     a. sentence 1
     b. sentence 2
     c. sentence 3
     d. sentence 5

_____3. The major points of this passage will most likely explain _____.
     a. how to become a participant on television game shows
     b. how to succeed in television game shows
     c. the terms used by psychologists who study memory
     d. the experiments utilized by psychologists who study memory

_____4. Sentence 10 serves as a _____ for the passage.
     a. central theme
     b. topic
     c. major detail for the passage
     d. minor supporting detail for a major detail

_____5. How many major points support the central idea of this passage?
     a. one
     b. three
     c. five
     d. seven

6–10. Fill in the outline by completing the major and minor details that are missing.

Retention and Relearning

0. (6)_____

     a. (7)_____

     b. (8)_____

     c. Paired associate tasks

     d. *The Weakest Link*, fill-in-the-blank questions, and essay tests use recall.

1. (9)_____

     a. Requires recognizing information

     b. *Who wants to Be a Millionaire?* and multi-choice tests use recognition.

2. (10)_____

     a. Measures how long it takes to relearn material

     b. Rapid relearning indicates residual memory.

Name_____ Section _____ Date _____ Score (number correct) _____ x 10 = _____

Directions: Read the paragraphs and answer the questions that follow.

[1]By the time the average infant has reached the age of 1 year, it has tripled its birth weight and added about another foot to its height. [2]The brain triples its weight in the firsts two years, reaching about 75 percent of its adult weight. [3]By age 5, the brain is at 90 percent of its adult weight. [4]This increase makes possible a tremendous amount of major advances in cognitive development, including the development of thinking, problem, solving, and memory.

[5]One way of examining the development of cognition is found in the work of Jean Piaget. [6]Piaget proposed that there are four distinct stages of cognitive development that occur from infancy to adolescence.

[7]The sensorimotor stage is the first of Piaget's stages. [8]It concerns infants from birth to age 2. [9]In this stage, infants use their senses and motor abilities to learn about the world around them. [10]They begin to interact deliberately with objects by grasping, pushing, tasting, and so on.

[11]Next is the preoperational stage (ages 2-7). [12]This is a time of developing language and concepts. [13]Children can now ask questions and explore their surroundings more fully. [14]However, they are not yet capable of logical thought—they can use simple mental concepts but are not able to use those concepts in a more rational, logical sense. [15]For example, it doesn't occur to them to think about how Santa Claus might get to every child's house in one night, or how he gets inside, especially when there is no chimney.

[16]In the concrete operational stage (ages 7-12), children finally become capable of conservation and reversible thinking. [17]Although children begin to think more logically and rationally, they are unable to deal effectively with abstract concepts. [18]Children at this stage need to be able to see touch, or at least see in their heads an object in order to understand it.

[19]Formal operational (ages 12 to adulthood) is the last of Piaget's stages. [20]Abstract thinking now becomes possible. [21]Teenagers not only understand concepts that have no physical reality, but also they get deeply involved in hypothetical thinking or thinking about possibilities and even impossibilities. [22]"What if everyone just got along?" [23]"If women were in charge of countries, would there be fewer wars?"

—Adapted from Ciccarelli and White, *Psychology*, 2nd ed., pp. 325–328.

_____1. The topic this passage is _____.
    a. stages of growth
    b. cognitive development
    c. tracing a life-span
    d. analyzing the thinking brain

_____2. The central idea is stated in _____.
    a. sentence 1
    b. sentence 2
    c. sentence 4
    d. sentence 6

____3. The central idea of the passage is supported by _____.
  a. examples of cognitive abilities at each stage
  b. statistics that demonstrate differences in development
  c. testimony by noted child psychologists
  d. journal articles that confirm the information

____4. Sentences 7, 11, 16, and 19 serve as _____?
  a. central themes
  b. main ideas
  c. major supporting details
  d. minor supporting details

____5. Sentences 22 and 23 serve as _____ for the paragraph?
  a. central themes
  b. main ideas
  c. major supporting details
  d. minor supporting details

6-10. Fill in the outline by completing the major and minor details that are missing.

Piaget's Stages of Development

1. (6)_____

  a. Birth to 2 years of age

  b. Development of senses and motor ability

2. Preoperational stage

  a. (7)_____

  b. Development of language and concepts

  c. Lacks ability to think logically

3. (8)_____
    a. Ages 7 – 12 years of age

  b. Development of conservation and reversible thinking

  c. Lacks ability to deal effectively with abstract concepts

4. (9)_____

  a. (10) _____

  b. Development of abstract thinking

Name_____ Section _____ Date _____ Score (number correct) _____ x 10 = _____

Directions: Read the paragraphs and answer the questions that follow.

Paragraph A

[1]According to cultivation theory, the media, especially television, are the main means by which you learn about your society and your culture: What you watch and how often you watch it will influence your views of the world and people. [2]Cultivation theory argues that heavy television viewers form an image of reality that is in conflict with the facts. [3]For example, heavy viewers see their chances of being a victim of crime to be 1 in 10, yet in reality the ratio is 1 in 50. [4]Heavy viewers also think that 20 percent of the world's population lives in the United States; however, in reality it's only 6 percent. [5]Furthermore, heavy viewers believe that the percentage of workers in managerial or professional jobs is 25 percent; in reality, it's 5 percent.

—Adapted from De Vito, *The Interpersonal Communication Book,* 10th ed., p. 107.

1.   The topic of this paragraph is
        a.   the media
        b.   television views
        c.   television viewing habits
        d.   cultivation theory

2.   The main idea of the paragraph is stated in _____.
        a.   sentence 2
        b.   sentence 3
        c.   sentence 4
        d.   sentence 5

3.   The major details of this paragraph are intended to _____.
        a. explain why people view so much television
        b. provide examples of views that conflict with reality
        c. list the types of favorite television shows
        d. describe the studies used to measure television-viewing habits

4.   Sentence 2 serves as a _____ for the paragraph.
        a.   main idea
        b.   major supporting detail
        c.   minor supporting detail
        d.   specific example

5.   Which words in the paragraph signal the major supporting details?
        a.   *according to*
        b.   *what you watch*
        c.   *for example, also,* and *furthermore*
        d.   *cultivation* and *media*

Paragraph B

[1]Moral theories provide different frameworks through which nurses can view and clarify disturbing client care situations. [2]Three types of moral theories are widely used, and they can be differentiated by their emphasis on (a) consequences, (b) principles and duties, or (c) relationships. [3]Consequence-based theories look to the outcomes of an action in judging whether that action is right or wrong. [4]For instance a nurse might judge a good act as one that brings the most benefit and the least harm for the greatest number of people. [5]The second type, principle-based theories, involve logical and formal processes and emphasize individual rights, duties, and obligations. [6]For example, following the rule "Do not lie," a nurse might believe he or she should tell the truth to a dying client, even though the physician has given instruction not to do so. [7]Last, relationship-based theories stress courage, generosity, and commitment. [8]The need to nurture and maintain relationships is very important. [9]Caring theories, for example, allow nurses to judge actions according to a perspective of caring and responsibility.

—Adapted from Kozier and Erb, *Fundamentals of Nursing: Concepts, Process, and Practice,* 8th ed., p. 84.

6.   The main idea of the paragraph is stated in _____.
        a. sentence 1
        b. sentence 2
        c. sentence 3
        d. sentence 5

7.   The major points of this passage will most likely explain _____.
        a. difficult issues in nursing
        b. the three types of moral theories
        c. comparisons among nursing jobs
        d. causes of nursing burnout

8–10.   Fill in the outline by completing the major and minor details that are missing.

Moral Theories

1. _(8)_____
        a. Look to the outcomes of an action in to make judgments
        b. For example, a good act brings the most benefit and least harm

2. _(9)_____
        a. involve logical and formal processes and emphasize individual rights, duties, and obligations
        b. For example, telling the truth is more important.

3. Relationship-based theories
        a. (10)_____
        b. For example, allow nurses to judge actions according to a perspective of caring and responsibility.

91

Name_____ Section _____ Date _____ Score (number correct) _____ x 10 = _____

Directions: Read the paragraph and answer the questions that follow.

Technological Development

[1]Technological progress begins with two factors. [2]The first factor is discovery. [3]Discovery is learning something that was not known before about the physical or social world. [4]For example, in the past, explorers have discovered new islands. [5]Astronauts have uncovered some of the laws that control the universe. [6]Invention is the second factor of technological progress. [7]An invention is a new way of doing something or a new object or mechanical device created to serve some specific purpose. [8]Inventions may be either material or nonmaterial. [9]For example, machines such as the automobile and airplane are material inventions. [10]Insurance and crop rotation are nonmaterial inventions. [11]One of the greatest of all nonmaterial inventions was the alphabet; it has made possible our present system of writing and printing.

—Adapted from Hunt & Colander, *Social Science*, 11th ed., p. 85.

_____1. The topic of this paragraph is
    a. discovery
    b. technological development
    c. great scientists
    d. inventions

_____2. The main idea of the paragraph is stated in _____.
    a. sentence 1
    b. sentence 3
    c. sentence 6
    d. sentence 11

_____3. In general, the supporting details of this paragraph _____.
    a. offer praise for explorers and inventors
    b. explain the need for funding of research
    c. explain the traits of discoveries and inventions and give examples
    d. list famous inventions

_____4. Sentence 2 serves as a _____ for the paragraph.
    a. main idea
    b. major supporting detail
    c. minor supporting detail
    d. irrelevant fact

_____5. Sentence 4 serves as a _____ for the paragraph.
    a. main idea
    b. major supporting detail
    c. minor supporting detail
    d. specific example

____6. How many major supporting details are in this paragraph?
        a. two
        b. three
        c. four
        d. five

____7. What word or phrase signals the first major supporting detail?
        a. first
        b. one
        c. for example
        d. beginning with

____8. What word or phrase signals the second major supporting detail?
        a. and
        b. next
        c. second

        d. for example

Directions: Use the concept map for questions 9 and 10.

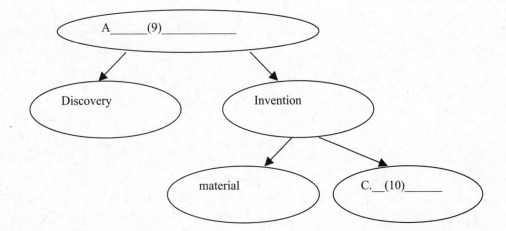

_____9. What word or phrase should complete part A of the concept map?
- a. the first factor
- b. discovery
- c. laws that control the universe
- d. technological progress

_____10. What word or phrase should complete part C of the concept map?
- a. factor
- b. technological progress
- c. nonmaterial
- d. the alphabet

Name_____ Section _____ Date _____ Score (number correct) _____ x 10 = _____

Objective: To use time and pace order transitions to see the relationship of details to the main idea

A. Directions: Read the paragraphs and insert the appropriate transition from the box on the numbered

once	next	first	then	beginning

lines.

Check into any Ritz-Carlton hotel around the world, and you'll be amazed by the company's dedication to anticipating and meeting even your slightest need. Without ever asking, they seem to know that you want a king-size bed, a nonallergencic pillow, and breakfast with decaffeinated coffee in your room the (___1___) morning. From the (___2___) day, those at the front desk to those in maintenance and housekeeping discreetly observe and record even the smallest guest preferences.

At the (___3___) of every morning, each hotel reviews the files of all new arrivals who have stayed previously at a Ritz-Carlton and prepares a list of suggested extra touches that might delight each guest.

And (___4___) they identify a special customer need, The Ritz-Carlton employees go to legendary extremes to meet it. For example, to serve the needs of a guest with food allergies, a Ritz-Carlton chef in Bali located special eggs and milk in a small grocery store in another country and (___5___) had them delivered to the hotel.

—Adapted from Kotler and Armstrong, *Principles of Marketing*, 13th ed., p. 15.

B. Directions: Select the suitable transition word or expression to complete each sentence adapted from a college psychology textbook.

—Adapted from Ciccarelli and White, *Psychology*, 2nd ed., p. 583.

____6.   Although all people with schizophrenia share symptoms, the way in which these symptoms show up in behavior can be used to distinguish among several different _____ of schizophrenia.
   a.   spaces
   b.   times
   c.   associations
   d.   types

95

____7. There are five basic _____ of schizophrenia.
         a. contrasts
         e. categories
         f. lists
         g. additions

____8. One _____ of schizophrenia is *disorganized* schizophrenia. These people are very confused in speech, have vivid and frequent hallucinations, and tend to have very inappropriate emotions.
         a. then
         b. during
         c. kind
         d. behind

____9. Although it is becoming rare, *catatonic* schizophrenia is a _____ type of schizophrenia that involves very disturbed motor behavior. The person doesn't respond to the outside world and either doesn't move at all, maintaining often odd-looking postures for hours on end, or moves about wildly in great agitation.
         a. previous
         b. category
         c. next
         d. second

____10. _____, people diagnosed with *paranoid* schizophrenia suffer from hallucinations and delusions. Auditory hallucinations are common, and the delusions are typically persecution, grandeur, or extreme jealousy.
         a. finally
         b. then
         c. when
         d. another

Name_____ Section _____ Date _____ Score (number correct) _____ x 10 = _____

Objective: To use addition transitions and the listing pattern to see the relationship of details to the main idea.

A. Directions: Choose a word from the box to fill in the blanks with transitions that show the relationship between ideas.

also	as well as	furthermore	including
and	first	in addition	yet

Doug Williams leads me to his room of baseball memorabilia with a puckish grin that belies his age. A (1_____) glance around the room reveals baseball jerseys, bats, hats, (2_____) posters, (3_____) autographed balls and gloves that line the shelves and walls. A meticulous collector, Doug has each item mentally cataloged, but he has (4_____) arranged items in notebooks and scrapbooks and journals. While the collecting began with baseball cards, it quickly advanced to other items, (5_____) gloves and autographed balls.

B. Directions: Read the paragraphs and answer the questions that follow

Colors may communicate different meanings based on how they are viewed in various cultures. One example is the color red. In China red signifies wealth, success, and rebirth. In many African countries it represents death, and in Japan, it means anger and danger. Another example is green. In the United States green signifies money or envy. Among some Native Americans it is a sign of femininity. And to the Egyptians it communicates fertility and strength.

—Adapted from De Vito, *The Interpersonal Communication Book*, 10th ed., p. 203.

_____ 6.   The second major supporting detail is signaled by the transition word _____.
      a. different
      b. one
      c. another
      d. and

_____7. The thought pattern used in the paragraph is
     a. listing.
     b. time pattern.

There was virtually no daily press when the United States Constitution was written. The daily newspaper is largely a product of the mid-nineteenth century; radio and television have been around only since the first half of the twentieth century. As recently as the presidency of Herbert Hoover (1929–1933), reporters submitted their questions to the president in writing, and he responded in writing—if at all. Hoover's successor, Franklin D. Roosevelt (1935–1945), practically invented media politics. To Roosevelt, the media were a potential ally. Roosevelt promised reporters two press conferences a week during his 12 years in the White House. This relatively cozy relationship between politicians and the press lasted through the early 1960s. The events of the Vietnam War, however, soured the press on government. Today's newspeople work in an environment of cynicism. To them, politicians rarely tell the whole story; the press sees ferreting out the truth as their job.

—Adapted from Edwards, Wattenberg, and Lineberry,
Government in America: People, Politics, and Policy, 13th ed., pp. 213–215.

_____8. The overall thought pattern for the paragraph is_____.
     a. time order
     b. listing
     c. space order
     d. classification

[1]Currently there are seven known forms of hepatitis, with hepatitis A, B, and C having the highest rates of incidence. [2]In the United States, hepatitis continues to be a major threat in spite of a safe blood supply and massive efforts at education about hand washing and safer sex. [3]Several of these _____ of hepatitis have reached epidemic proportions among certain segments of the population.

—Donatelle, *Access to Health,* 10th ed., p. 520.

_____9. The transition word that best fits the blank in sentence 3 is _____.
     a. characteristics
     b. frequently
     c. forms
     d. epidemics

_____10. The thought pattern used in the paragraph is
     a. time order.
     b. space order.
     c. listing.
     d. classification.

Name _____ Section _____ Date _____ Score (number correct) _____ x 10 = _____

Directions: Read the paragraphs and answer the questions that follow.

Paragraph A

[1]Helen Fisher is a researcher at the American Museum of Natural History and an author on the topic of love, adultery and divorce. [2]In her studies, she has attempted to shed light on the process of falling in love. [3]According to Fisher, attraction and falling in love follow a pattern based on several factors. [4] The _____ factor in the pattern is imprinting. [5]Imprinting means that our genetic makeup and past experiences trigger a romantic reaction. [6]The next aspect of the pattern is attraction. [7]Attraction may be linked to chemicals in our bodies that produce feelings of euphoria and elation. [8]And a _____ factor is attachment. [9] Endorphins (natural opiates) cause lovers to feel peaceful, secure, and calm.

—Adapted from Donatelle, *Access to Health*, 7th ed., p. 133.

_____ 1. The main idea of this paragraph is expressed in _____.
     a. sentence 1
     b. sentence 2
     c. sentence 3
     d. sentence 4

_____ 2. The transition word that best fits the blank in sentence 4 is _____.
     a. *next*
     b. *frequently*
     c. *first*
     d. *additional*

_____ 3. The transition word that best fits the blank in sentence 8 is _____.
     a. *moreover*
     b. *frequently*
     c. *third*
     d. *additional*

_____ 4. The thought pattern used in the paragraph is _____.
     a. time order.
     b. space order
     c. listing
     d. classification

_____ 5. The transition words that signal the pattern of thought are _____.
     a. *in*, *according*, and *the*
     b. *researcher* and *author*
     c. *first*, *next*, and *third*
     d. *attraction* and *endorphins*

Paragraph B

[1]One group of students with special needs is often overlooked in schools: the gifted and talented. [2]A national survey found that more than one-half of all gifted students do not achieve in school at a level equal to their ability. [3]Individuals can have many _____ of gifts. [4]Some experts have defined giftedness as a combination of three basic _____. [5]One is an above-average general ability. [6]A _____ consists of a high level of creativity, and the third trait that marks a gifted student is a high level of commitment or motivation to achieve.

—Adapted from Woolfolk, *Educational Psychology*, 8th ed., pp. 122–123.

_____6.   The main idea of this paragraph is found in _____.
    a.   sentence 3
    b.   sentence 4
    c.   sentence 5
    d.   sentence 6

_____7.   The appropriate transition word for the blank in sentence 3 is _____.
    a.   *group*
    b.   *types*
    c.   *second*
    d.   *trait*

_____8.   The appropriate transition word for the blank in sentence 4 is _____.
    a.   *moreover*
    b.   *characteristics*
    c.   *stages*
    d.   *kind*

_____9.   The appropriate transition word for the blank in sentence 6 is _____.
    a.   *one*
    b.   *second*
    c.   *in addition*
    d.   *and*

_____10.   The primary thought pattern used in this paragraph is _____
    a.   time order
    b.   space order
    c.   listing
    d.   classification

Name _____ Section _____ Date _____ Score (number correct) _____ x 10 = _____

Directions: Read the paragraphs and answer the questions that follow.

1 __(1)__ the 1970s, psychologists used the term *short-term memory* to refer to memory that lasts for less than a minute. However, in the 1970s, researchers Alan Baddeley and Graham Hitch __(2)__ to rethink short-term memory as a more complex type of brief storage they called *working memory*. Their model contains several levels that operate simultaneously to maintain information __(3)__ it is being processed. Earlier psychologists often concentrated on single memory tasks, trying to understand the various stages of how a single task was processed in the brain. But the concept of working memory goes beyond individual stages to describe the active integration of both conscious processes (such as repetition) and unconscious processes. This current model of memory emphasizes how human memory meets the demands of real-life activities such as listening to the radio while reading, and mentally calculating the sum of 74 plus 782 all at the same time.

2 The addition of new information may *interfere* with the recall of other information in working memory. Baddeley and Hitch demonstrated the limited capabilities of several components, or subsystems, of working memory by having participants recall digits while doing some other type of reasoning task. If one subsystem is given a demanding task, the performance of the others will suffer. One subsystem in working memory encodes, rehearses, and holds auditory information such as a person's name or phone number. __(4)__ subsystem is a visual-spatial scratch pad or blackboard, which stores visual and spatial information, such as the appearance and location of objects, for a brief time and then is erased to allow new information to be stored. A third subsystem is a central processing mechanism, something like an executive who balances the information flow and allows people to solve problems and make decisions. This executive controls the processing flow and adjusts it when necessary. Research shows that the type of information being processed by working memory affects the accuracy of the processing. For example, reading a passage consisting entirely of words presents different requirements from reading a passage with both words and pictures, and the central processing mechanism must make adjustments for the different types of information being processed.

3 Unlike the working memory, information about names, faces, dates, places, smells, and events is stored in relatively permanent form in *long-term memory*. __(5)__ to the limitations of sensory and short-term storage, long-term memory is indefinite; much of it lasts a lifetime. The capacity of long-term memory also seems unlimited; the more information a person acquires, the easier it is to acquire more information. Using our filing cabinet analogy, we can say that long-term memory includes all the folders in the cabinet. And as in a filing cabinet, information can be lost ("misfiled") or unavailable for some other reason (the drawers can get stuck). Different from a filing cabinet, however, the information in human memory is active rather than passive in storage and subject to distortion—as if the memos in the folder had morphed into photographs of the office staff while in the cabinet.

—Adapted from Lefton & Brannon, *Psychology,* 8th ed., pp. 272–273.

_____1.   The transition word that best fits blank 1 in the first paragraph is _____.
  a. next
  b. often
  c. until
  d. additional

_____2.   The transition word that best fits blank 2 in the first paragraph is _____.
  a. began
  b. often
  c. until
  d. additional

_____3.   The transition word that best fits blank 3 in the first paragraph is _____.
  a. began
  b. often
  c. until
  d. while

_____4.   Transition words such as *until, in the 1970s, earlier,* and *often* that appear in the first paragraph indicate _____.
  a. comparison
  b. time
  c. classification
  d. listing

_____5.   The transition word that best fits blank 4 in the second paragraph is _____.
  a. frequently
  b. also
  c. another
  d. later

_____6.   Transition words such as *several, one,* and *third* that appear in the second paragraph indicate
_____.
  a. time order
  b. space order
  c. listing
  d. contrast

_____7.   . How many major supporting details support the main idea of the second paragraph?
  a. one
  b. two
  c. three
  d. four

_____8.   The transition word that best fits blank 5 in the third paragraph is _____.
  a. frequently
  b. in contrast
  c. another
  d. later

_____9. Transition words such as *unlike, different from,* and *however* that appear in the third paragraph indicate _____.

       a. time order

       b. space order

       c. listing

       d. contrast

_____10. The topic of the entire passage is _____.

       a. memory

       b. short-term memory

       c. working memory

       d. conscious and unconscious processes

Name _____ Section _____ Date _____ Score (number correct) _____ x 10 = _____

Directions: Read the paragraphs and answer the questions that follow.

A. [1]To find order in the diversity of life, biologists have long sought ways to categorize living things. [2]In 1969 a classification system of *five kingdoms* was proposed. [3]In this system the fundamental criteria for classifying organisms are the presence or absence of a nucleus, the number of cells, and the type of metabolism. [4]In recent years new techniques in molecular biology and biochemistry have caused many biologists to advocate another classification system that begins with domains, a higher classification level that encompasses kingdoms. [5]In this system, organisms are distributed across domains, each comprising a kingdom. [6]Other classification systems have been proposed, including systems with five, seven, and eight kingdoms. [7]All these systems are subject to change as new information is discovered.

—Adapted from Johnson, *Human Biology: Concepts and Current Issues*, 5th ed., pp. 4–5.

_____1. The main idea of this paragraph is expressed in _____.
     a. sentence 1
     b. sentence 2
     c. sentence 3
     d. sentence 4

_____2. Which transitions signal the thought pattern of this paragraph?
     a. *system* and *fundamental*
     b. *in 1969* and *recent*
     c. *another* and *other*
     d. *categorize* and *classification*

_____3. How many major details support the main idea in this paragraph?
     a. one
     b. two
     c. three
     d. four

_____4. In general, the major details of this paragraph _____.
     a. list categories that classify living organisms
     b. explain the characteristics of cell types
     c. analyze the discoveries of molecular biology
     d. depict the structure of cells

_____5. The thought pattern used in the paragraph is _____.
     a. comparison-contrast
     b. process
     c. generalization and example
     d. classification

Directions: Read the following paragraph from a college psychology textbook. Transition words are highlighted in **bold** type. Identify the type of transition for each of these words, and then answer the final question.

B. The goal of preventing psychological problems can be realized at several different points. The **first** point, primary prevention, seeks to put a stop to a condition **before** it begins. Steps might be taken, for example, to teach people healthy coping skills. At the same time, primary prevention may also seek to change the situations that lead to mental problems such as anxiety or depression. Next is secondary prevention. In secondary prevention, attempts are made to limit the length and difficulty of a disorder **once** it has begun. Programs that allow for early identification and prompt treatment of problems help achieve this goal. **Finally**, tertiary prevention limits the longterm impact of a psychological disorder by seeing to avoid a relapse.

—Adapted from Gerrig & Zimbardo, *Psychology and Life*, 16th ed., p. 531.

_____6. The transition *first* signal _____.
   a. addition
   b. time
   c. space
   d. classification

_____7. The transition *before* signals _____.
   a. addition
   b. time
   c. space
   d. classification

_____8. The transition *once* signals _____.
   a. addition
   b. time
   c. space
   d. classification

_____9. The transition *finally* signals _____.
   a. addition
   b. time
   c. space
   d. classification

_____10. What is the overall thought pattern in the paragraph?
   a. listing
   b. time order
   c. space order
   d. classification

105

Name _____ Section _____ Date _____ Score (number correct) _____ x 10 = _____

Directions: Read the paragraphs and answer the questions that follow.

Paragraph A

[1]Special breathing techniques can decrease stress. [2]First, establish deep breathing from the diaphragm. [3]Then over a period of weeks, continue practicing deep breathing in order to reduce the number of breaths taken per minute. [4]_____ dealing with stressors, exhale, letting breath go slowly and deeply to reduce anxiety.

—Adapted from McGuigan, *Encyclopedia of Stress*, p. 37.

_____1. The relationship between sentence 2 and sentence 3 is one of
   a. time order
   b. listing
   c. space order
   d. classification

_____2. The transition that best fits the blank in sentence 4 is
   a. *After*
   b. *First*
   c. *When*
   d. *Finally*

Paragraph B

[1]Among mammals, only primates have full color vision. [2]A bull does not charge a red cape; he charges when he sees an annoying gray object being waved at him. [3]Among nonmammals, many birds and fishes also have excellent color vision; the brightly colored lure may really appeal to the fish as much as to the angler who bought it. [4]Most colors can be described in terms of three physical dimensions: wavelength, intensity, and purity. [5]_____, three perceptual dimensions, hue, brightness, and saturation, match the physical dimensions and help us describe what we see.

—Adapted from Carlson & Buskist, *Psychology: The Science of Behavior*, 5th ed., p. 175.

_____3. The relationship between sentence 2 and sentence 3 is one of
   a. time order
   b. listing
   c. space order
   d. classification

_____4. The transition that best fits the blank in sentence 5 is
   a. *Next*
   b. *Furthermore*
   c. *When*
   d. *Before*

Paragraph C

[1]When faithfully followed, these four steps should ensure mastery of the material you will face in an intermediate algebra class. [2]First, begin to study for the final exam three days to two weeks ahead of the exam. [3]Browse through each chapter, reviewing the important formulas. [4]If the textbook offers summaries and reviews, read these, too. [5]For step two, summarize all formulas on an index card and quiz yourself frequently. [6]As your third step, retake each chapter test that you took in class, assuming your instructor has returned it. [7]At this time, restudy the objectives in the text that go with each question that you missed. [8]Finally, for any remaining difficulties, see your instructor, go to a tutoring session, or join a study group.

—Adapted from Bittinger & Beecher, *Introductory and Intermediate Algebra,* 2nd ed., p. 892.

_____5. The topic of this paragraph is _____.
  a. mastery of material
  b. intermediate algebra class
  c. study tips for intermediate algebra
  d. steps for studying

_____6. The main idea is expressed in _____.
  a. sentence 1
  b. sentence 2
  c. sentence 4
  d. sentence 6

_____7. In general the main points of this paragraph _____.
  a. describe the difficulties of math classes
  b. classify the levels of math classes
  c. analyze the characteristics of students who perform poorly in math
  d. list the steps involved in mastering intermediate algebra

_____8. The relationship between sentence 6 and sentence 7 is one of _____.
  a. space order
  b. classification
  c. time order
  d. addition

_____9. The thought pattern used in the paragraph is
  a. classification
  b. listing
  c. time order
  d. space order

_____10. The transition words that signal this pattern are _____.
  a. *when faithfully follows*
  b. *these four steps*
  c. *on a regular basis*
  d. *use the chapter test*

107

Name_____ Section _____ Date _____ Score (number correct) _____ x 10 = _____

Objective: To use comparison and contrast transitions and thought patterns.

Directions: Choose the most appropriate transition to complete the sentence based upon the thought pattern that is expressed.

It is a struggle to learn a new culture, *for* the behaviors and ways of thinking contrast with the one already learned. This can lead to inner turmoil. *One* way to handle the conflict is to cut ties with your *first* culture. This, *however*, can create a sense of loss that is recognized only later in life.

—Henslin, *Essentials of Sociology,* 5th ed., p. 70.

_____1. Which italicized word indicates a comparison-and-contrast pattern?
     a. for
     b. one
     c. first
     d. however

Richard Rodriguez, a literature professor and essayist, was born *in* the 1950s to working-class Mexican immigrants. Wanting their son to be successful in their adopted land, his parents named him Richard *instead of* Ricardo. *While* his English-Spanish hybrid name indicates the parents' aspirations for their son, it was *also* an omen of the conflict Richard would experience.

—Henslin, *Essentials of Sociology,* 5th ed., p. 70.

_____2. Which italicized word indicates a comparison or a contrast?
     a. in
     b. instead of
     c. while
     d. also

Like other children of Mexican immigrants, Richard's *first* language was Spanish—a rich mother tongue that gave him his orientation to the world. *Until* the age of 5, when he began school, Richard knew only fifty words in English. He describes what happened *when* he began school:

The change came gradually but early. When I was beginning grade school, I noted to myself the fact that the classroom environment was so different in its styles and assumptions from my own family environment that survival would essentially entail a choice between both worlds. When I became a student, I was literally "remade"; neither I nor my teachers considered anything I had known before as relevant. I had to forget most of what my culture had provided, because to remember it was a disadvantage. The past and its cultural values became detachable, like a piece of clothing grown heavy on a warm day and finally put away.

—Henslin, *Essentials of Sociology,* 5th ed., p. 70.

108

_____3. Which italicized transition word indicates a comparison or a contrast?
   a. like
   b. first
   c. until
   d. when

_____4. According to Rodriguez, what was like a piece of clothing grown heavy on a warm day that was finally put away?
   a. giving up his dreams
   b. his connection to his culture
   c. learning math skills
   d. his connection to English literature

As happened to millions of immigrants before him, whose parents spoke German, Polish, Italian, and so on, learning English eroded family and class ties and ate away at his ethnic roots. For him, language and education were not simply devices that eased the transition to the dominant culture. Instead, they transformed Richard into a *pocho,* "a Mexican with gringo aspirations." They slashed at the roots that had given him life.

—Henslin, *Essentials of Sociology,* 5th ed., p. 70.

_____5. From this paragraph, you could conclude that learning English _____.
   a. destroyed some of his family relationships
   b. destroyed some of his connections to the working class and Mexican culture
   c. changed his dreams
   d. All of the above

_____6. Which culture does a *pocho* withdraw from?
   a. the old culture
   b. the new culture
   c. the Italian culture
   d. the American culture

To face such inner turmoil is to confront a fork in the road. Some turn one way and withdraw from the new culture—a clue that helps explain the high dropout rate of Latinos from U.S. schools. Others go in the opposite direction and, cutting ties with their family and cultural roots, wholeheartedly adopt the new culture.

—Henslin, *Essentials of Sociology,* 5th ed., p. 70.

_____7. The explanation for the high dropout rate of Latinos in U.S. schools is that some Latinos choose to cut ties with _____.
   a. their family
   b. their past and their old culture
   c. their new culture
   d. their first language

Rodriguez took the second road. He excelled in his new language—so well, in fact, that he graduated from Stanford University and then became a graduate student in English at the University of California at Berkeley. He was even awarded a prestigious Fulbright fellowship to study English Renaissance literature at the British Museum.

—Henslin, *Essentials of Sociology,* 5th ed., p. 70.

_____8. "Rodriguez took the second road" means that _____.
   a. he cut ties with the English language
   b. he cut ties with his new culture
   c. he cut ties with his ethnic roots
   d. he refused to excel in school

But the past wouldn't let Rodriguez alone. Prospective employers were impressed with his knowledge of Renaissance literature, but at job interviews they would ask if he would teach the Mexican novel in translation and be an adviser to Latino students. Rodriguez was haunted by the image of his grandmother, the warmth of the culture he had left behind, the language and thought to which he had become a stranger.

—Henslin, *Essentials of Sociology,* 5th ed., p. 70.

_____9. The transition word *but* indicates that Richard Rodriguez _____.
   a. returned to live permanently in Mexico
   b. missed his Mexican roots and wanted to reconnect to his first culture
   c. never found a job teaching English literature
   d. returned to Mexico to work for his father

Richard Rodriguez represents millions of immigrants—not just those of Latino origin but those from other cultures, too—who want to be a part of the United States without betraying their past. They fear that to integrate into U.S. culture is to lose their roots. They are caught between two cultures, each beckoning, each offering rich rewards.

—Henslin, *Essentials of Sociology,* 5th ed., p. 70.

_____10. The author compares Rodriguez to _____.
   a. other Latinos
   b. other immigrants
   c. people who fear coming to the United States
   d. people who choose not to leave their homeland

Name_____ Section _____ Date _____ Score (number correct) _____ x 10 = _____

Objective: To use transitions correctly and to identify patterns of thought.

Directions: Read the following paragraphs from a college social science textbook. Fill in the blanks in each paragraph with the appropriate transition words or phrases. Then answer the questions following the paragraph.

____1. [1]Definitions often reflect an attitude toward the thing that is being defined. [2]Words that describe hallucinogens_____ this point.
    a. as
    b. on the other hand
    c. illustrate
    d. compare

____2. [3]Those who view these drugs with a positive spin describe them _____ "mind-expanding" or "making the mind manifest."
    a. different from
    b. leading to
    c. as
    d. for example

____3. [4]_____, those who view these drugs with alarm describe them a "mind-disrupting" or "mind-dissolving." [5]You can see that the description one chooses to use carries a strong attitude, pro or con, toward the drug's effect.

          —Adapted from Levinthal, *Drugs, Behaviors, and Modern Society,* 3rd ed., p. 125.

    a. however
    b. result in
    c. subsequently
    d. including

____4. The relationship between sentence 1 and sentence 2 is
    a. cause and effect
    b. generalization and example
    c. comparison and contrast
    d. definition

____5. The relationship between sentence 3 and sentence 4 is
    a. cause and effect
    b. definition and example
    c. comparison and contrast
    d. generalization and example

111

____6. [1]The phrase "instrumental use of drugs" _____ that a person is taking a drug with a specific, socially approved goal in mind. [2]For example, the user may want to stay awake longer, fall asleep more quickly, or recover from an illness.
    a. in contrast
    b. means
    c. for example
    d. results in

____7. [3]_____, the phrase "recreational use of drugs" means that a person is taking the drug for the purpose of having the effect of the drug itself. [4]For example, the user wants to enjoy a feeling or state of mind. [5]The term *misuse* typically applies to cases in which a drug is used inappropriately.
    a. for example
    b. in contrast
    c. means
    d. leads to

____8. [6]Many instances of drug misuse involve instrumental goals. [7]_____, drug doses may be increased beyond the level of the prescription in the mistaken idea that if a little is good, then more is even better. [8]Or doses may be decreased from the level of the prescription to make the drug supply last longer. [9]Drug misuse can lead to serious complications and even death.

        —Adapted from Levinthal, *Drugs, Behaviors, and Modern Society,* 3rd ed., pp. 4–5.

    a. for instance
    b. meaning
    c. because
    d. in contrast

____9. The relationship between sentence 1 and sentence 2 is _____.
    a. cause and effect
    b. definition and example
    c. comparison and contrast
    d. generalization and example

____10. The relationship between sentence 6 and sentence 7 is _____.
    a. cause and effect
    b. generalization and example
    c. comparison
    d. contrast

Name_____ Section _____ Date _____ Score (number correct) _____ x 10 = _____

Directions: Read each of the following sentences and identify the pattern of thought as indicated by the transitions.

_____1. Compulsive gambling is an example of a mental disorder.
      a. generalization and example
      b. comparison
      c. cause and effect
      d. definition and example

_____2. Effective communication skills lead to healthier relationships.
      a. cause and effect
      b. comparison
      c. generalization and example
      d. contrast

_____3. Listening and hearing differ in significant ways.
      a. definition and example
      b. contrast
      c. cause and effect
      d. comparison

Directions: Read the following paragraph and answer the questions that follow.

[1]Both President Ford and President Carter were men of decency and integrity, but neither earned a reputation as a strong, dynamic leader. [2]Although many Americans admired each man's honesty and sincerity, neither had the full confidence of the American people. [3]Moreover, neither leader had a clear sense of direction. [4]Both Ford and Carter seemed to waffle on major issues of public policy. [5]As a result, both became thought of as unsure, indecisive presidents. [6]For example, Ford began his term by urging tax increases, but later he called for a large tax cut. [7]Similarly, early on, Carter spoke of cutting military spending. [8]However, by the end of his term, he had come to support the idea of increasing defense spending.

—Adapted from Martin et al., *America and Its Peoples:
A Mosaic in the Making,* 3rd ed., pp. 1087–1088.

_____4. The phrase *but neither* in sentence 1 signals _____
      a. definition
      b. comparison
      c. contrast
      d. cause and effect

113

_____5. The phrase *although* in sentence 2 signals _____
      a.   definition
      b.   comparison
      c.   contrast
      d.   cause and effect

_____6. The transition *both* in sentence 4 signals _____.
      a.   definition
      b.   comparison
      c.   contrast
      d.   cause and effect

_____7. The transition *as a result* in sentence 5 signals _____.
      a.   definition
      b.   comparison
      c.   contrast
      d.   cause and effect

_____8. The relationship between sentence 6 and sentence 7 is _____.
      a.   definition
      b.   comparison
      c.   contrast
      d.   cause and effect

_____9. The relationship between sentence 7 and sentence 8 is _____.
      a.   definition
      b.   comparison
      c.   contrast
      d.   cause and effect

_____10. The primary pattern of thought in this paragraph is _____.
      a.   definition
      b.   comparison and contrast
      c.   generalization and example
      d.   cause and effect

Name_____Section_____Date_____Score (number correct)_____ x 10 = _____

Directions: Read each of the following sentences and identify the pattern of thought as indicated by the transitions.

_____1. PepsiCo is an example of a conglomerate, a giant corporation composed of many smaller corporations.
      a. generalization and example
      b. comparison
      c. cause and effect
      d. definition and example

_____2. The consequences of failing to read assignments before a class will be poor quiz grades.
      a. cause and effect
      b. comparison
      c. generalization and example
      d. contrast

_____3. Psychologists and psychiatrists differ in the nature and amount of education they have.
      a. definition and example
      b. contrast
      c. cause and effect
      d. comparison

Directions: Read the paragraphs below and answer the questions that follow.

The means by which a communication is presented—its medium—influences people's receptiveness to attitude change. Today, one of the most common avenues for attempts at attitude change is the mass media, particularly television. After all, the goal of TV commercials is either to change or to reinforce people's behavior. Commercials exhort viewers to drink Pepsi instead of Coke, to say no to drugs, or to vote for a Democrat *instead of* a Republican. Research shows that TV advertising is one of the most influential media for changing attitudes in the Western world; this is not too surprising, given the fact that the television is on for more than 4 hours every day in the average American household.

Nevertheless, face-to-face communication often has more impact than communication through television or in writing. Thus, even though candidates for public office rely heavily on TV, radio, and printed ads, they also try to meet people face to face, sometimes taking bus or train tours to deliver their message directly to the people.

      —Lefton & Brannon, *Psychology,* 8th ed., pp. 445–446.

_____4. A key word in the first sentence of this paragraph that signals a cause-and-effect pattern is _____.
      a. communication
      b. medium
      c. people's
      d. influences

115

_____5. According to the paragraph, what has the most persuasive effect?
      a. television
      b. radio
      c. face-to-face contact
      d. a well-designed Web site

_____6. According to the first paragraph, the desired effect of TV commercials is _____.
      a. to entertain audience
      b. to provide breaks
      c. to change behavior
      d. to persuade voters

_____7. The relationship between the second and first paragraph is one of _____.
      a. definition
      b. comparison
      c. contrast
      d. cause and effect

_____8. The transition word that indicates the relationship between the second and first paragraph is
_____.
      a. *often*
      b. *nevertheless*
      c. *thus*
      d. *also*

_____9. Of the transition words in the second paragraph, which indicates a cause-and-effect pattern in the second paragraph?
      a. *instead of*
      b. *nevertheless*
      c. *thus*
      d. *also*

_____10. The primary pattern of thought of this passage is _____.
      a. definition
      b. comparison and contrast
      c. generalization and example
      d. cause and effect

CHAPTER 8: MORE THOUGHT PATTERNS
Lab 8.5 MASTERY TEST 1

Name _____ Section _____ Date _____ Score (number correct) _____ x 10 = _____

Objective: To use transitions correctly and to identify patterns of thought.

A. Directions: Read each of the following sentences and identify the pattern of thought.

1.   Although many differences exist between the first child and the only child, some similarities can also be seen.
        a.   generalization and example
        b.   comparison
        c.   cause and effect
        d.   definition and example

2.   Sleep deprivation can result in chronic fatigue syndrome.
        a.   cause and effect
        b.   comparison
        c.   generalization and example
        d.   contrast

3.   Abraham Lincoln is an illustration of a man who suffered great inner conflict.
        a.   cause and effect
        b.   comparison
        c.   generalization and example
        d.   contrast

B. Directions: Read the following paragraphs and answer the questions that follow.

[1]Procrastination, the act of putting things off to the last minute, results in increased stress and lowered performance. For instance, Shayla put off starting her research paper until two days before it was due. [3]Within 48 hours, she had to find a topic, track down sources for the topic, read and take notes, write, revise, and proofread. [4]Her stress level went up as she discovered that she had to look up the rules for documenting her sources. [5]Because she had so many tasks to complete, she did not produce a quality paper.

_____ 4. The phrase *for instance* in sentence 2 signals _____.
        a.   an example
        b.   a comparison
        c.   a contrast
        d.   a cause and effect

_____ 5. The relationship between sentence 4 and sentence 5 is one of _____.
        a.   cause and effect
        b.   comparison
        c.   generalization and example
        d.   contrast

117

____6.   The primary pattern of organization for the paragraph is _____.
      a.   cause and effect
      b.   comparison
      c.   generalization and example
      d.   contrast

C. . Directions: Read the following paragraphs and answer the questions that follow.

[1]**Psychometrics** is the field of psychology that specializes in the mental testing in any of its facets. [2]This includes personality assessment, intelligence evaluation, and aptitude measurement. [3]The goal of psychometrics is to identify the basic psychological dimensions of the concept being investigated. [4]For example, one psychologist has determined that general intelligence can be broken down into two independent components, which he calls crystallized and fluid intelligence. [5]**Crystallized intelligence** involves the knowledge a person has already acquired and the ability to access that knowledge; it is measured by tests of vocabulary, arithmetic, and general information. [6]**Fluid intelligence** is the ability to see complex relationships and solve problems; it is measured by tests of block designs and spatial visualization.

—Adapted from Gerrig, and Zimbardo, *Psychology and Life,* 18th ed., p. 282.

____7. The word *psychometrics* followed by *is* in sentence 1 signals _____.
      a.   a definition
      b.   comparisons
      c.   examples
      d.   causes and effects

____8. The transition *includes* in sentence 2 signals that _____ will follow.
      a.   examples
      b.   comparisons
      c.   contrasts
      d.   causes and effects

____9. The purpose of sentence 4 is to provide a(n) _____ for the previous point.
      a.   definition
      b.   comparison
      c.   example
      d.   cause and effect

____10. The primary pattern of thought in this paragraph is _____.
      a.   definition and example
      b.   comparison and contrast
      c.   generalization and example
      d.   cause and effect

Name_____ Section _____ Date _____ Score (number correct) _____ x 10 = _____

Objective: To use transitions correctly and to identify patterns of thought.

A. Directions: Read each of the following sentences and identify the pattern of thought.

1.   A hero is a person willing to give up everything for the sake of another, expecting nothing in
      return. Many of the nation's firefighters embody such heroism.
          a. cause and effect
          b. definition and example
          c. comparison and contrast
          d. generalization and example

2.   Research remains unclear on the effects of media on the violent behavior of young people.
          a. cause and effect
          b. definition and example
          c. comparison and contrast
          d. generalization and example

3.   The main character in the short story "A Rose for Emily" by William Faulkner and the main
      character in "The Yellow Wallpaper" by Charlotte Perkins Gilman both struggle with insanity.
          a. cause and effect
          b. definition and example
          c. comparison and contrast
          d. generalization and example

4.   "All my friends do it" is an example of a kind of thinking called jumping on the bandwagon.
          a. cause and effect
          b. contrast
          c. comparison
          d. generalization and example

B. Directions: Read the following paragraphs and answer the questions that follow.

[1]To gain a better idea of what *social structure* is, think of college football. [2]You probably know the
various positions on the team: center, guards, tackles, ends, quarterback, running backs, and the like.
[3]Each is a *status;* that is, each is a social position with an expected role to attach to it. [4]The center is
expected to snap the ball, the quarterback to pass it, the guards to block, and so on. [5]Those *role
expectations* guide each player's actions; that is, the players try to do what their particular role requires.
[6]Even if you graduate and return five years later, the game will still be played, although the players have
changed.

119

[7]This scenario is very similar to *social structure*, the framework around which a group exists. [8]In this football example, that framework consists of the coaching staff and the eleven playing positions. [9]When someone leaves a position, the game can go on because someone else takes over that position or status and plays the role.

[10]Even though you may not play football, you nevertheless live your life within a clearly established social structure. [11]The statuses you occupy and the roles you play were already in place before you were born. [12]You take your particular positions in life, others do the same, and society goes about its business. [13]Although the specifics change with time, the game—whether of life or of football—goes on.

—Henslin, *Essentials of Sociology,* 5th ed., p. 85.

____5. The transition *similar* in sentence 7 signals _____.
   a. definition
   b. comparison
   c. example
   d. cause and effect

____6. An example of social structure are provided by _____.
   a. role expectations
   b. college graduates
   c. a college football team
   d. frameworks

____7. The relationship of sentence 8 to sentence 7 is one of _____.
   a. comparison
   b. contrast
   c. example
   d. cause and effect

____8. The transition *because* in sentence 9 signals that _____ will follow.
   a. definition
   b. comparison
   c. contrast
   d. causes and effect

____9. The transition *although* in sentence 13 signals _____.
   a. definition
   b. contrast
   c. example
   d. cause and effect

____10. The primary pattern of thought in this paragraph is _____.
   a. definition and example
   b. comparison and contrast
   c. generalization and example
   d. cause and effect

120

Name_____ Section _____ Date _____ Score (number correct) _____ x 10 = _____

Objective: To identify an author's use of facts and opinions in reading passages.

Directions: Read the statements and decide if they are facts, opinions, or a combination of fact and opinion.

_____ 1. Upon entering college, freshmen must take an English proficiency test to determine their readiness for college-level writing.
   a. fact
   b. opinion
   c. combination of fact and opinion

_____ 2. The horrific noise from the vuvuzela horns was extremely annoying to those watching the World Cup soccer games on television.
   a. fact
   b. opinion
   c. combination of fact and opinion

_____ 3. The Deepwater Horizon Oil Spill (caused by a drilling rig explosion in April 2010 in the Gulf of Mexico) is the largest offshore oil spill in U.S. history.
   a. fact
   b. opinion
   c. combination of fact and opinion

_____ 4. Michael Jackson, undisputed king of pop, is recognized as the most successful entertainer of all time by Guinness World Records.
   a. fact
   b. opinion
   c. combination of fact and opinion

_____ 5. Twilight is a series of four vampire-based fantasy romance novels that has everyone swooning over its brooding characters.
   a. fact
   b. opinion
   c. combination of fact and opinion

_____ 6. Proponents of the acai berry diet spout ridiculous claims and unsupported hype concerning its potential for miraculous weight-loss.
   a. fact
   b. opinion
   c. combination of fact and opinion

121

Directions: Read the following paragraph and answer the questions that follow.

[1]When you think of today's "hottest brands," what names come to mind? Coca-Cola? Nike? Google? [2]But scan last year's list of hottest brands, prepared by respected brand consultancy Landor Associates, and you'll find an unlikely entry—Las Vegas. [3]Most people wouldn't even think of Vegas as a "product," let alone as a brand. [4]But there it is, number two on the list of the nation's hottest brands, right behind Google. [5]Many old-timers still think of Las Vega a "Sin City"—an anything-goes gambling town. [6]Vegas was built on smoke-filled casinos, bawdy all-girl revues, all-you-can-eat buffets, Elvis impersonators, and no-wait weddings. [7]But that's the old Las Vegas. [8]The new Vegas has reinvented itself as a luxury destination. [9]Casinos and gaming now account for less than half of the city's revenues. [10]Instead, the new Las Vegas brims with classy resorts, expensive shopping malls, and gourmet restaurants.

—Adapted from Kotler and Armstrong, Principles of Marketing, 13th ed., p. 222.

_____ 7. Sentence 2 is an example of _____.
     a. fact
     b. opinion
     c. combination of fact and opinion

_____ 8. A biased word in sentence 2 is _____.
     a. *brands*
     b. *unlikely*
     c. *consultancy*
     d. *entry*

_____ 9. Sentence 3 is an example of _____.
     a. fact
     b. opinion
     c. combination of fact and opinion

_____ 10. A biased word in sentence 10 is _____.
     a. *instead*
     b. *resorts*
     c. *new*
     d. *classy*

CHAPTER 9: FACT AND OPINION
Lab 9.2 Practice Exercise 2

Name_____ Section _____ Date _____ Score (number correct) _____ x 10 = _____

Objective: To identify an author's use of facts and opinions in reading passages.

A. Directions: Read the statements and decide if they are facts, opinions, or a combination of fact and opinion.

____1. To fulfill graduation requirements, all students must take an introductory course in using computers or pass a computer competency test.
    a. fact
    b. opinion
    c. combination of fact and opinion

____2. Jill McCorkle, author of *Ferris Beach,* was only 26 in 1984 when she stunned the literary world by having two of her first novels published simultaneously.
    a. fact
    b. opinion
    c. combination of fact and opinion

____3. State lotteries exploit the poor, but they are an excellent way to generate revenue.
    a. fact
    b. opinion
    c. combination of fact and opinion

____4. *Crime and Punishment* is a novel by Russian author Fyodor Dostoevsky.
    a. fact
    b. opinion
    c. combination of fact and opinion

____5. If you can work through the Russian names, *Crime and Punishment* is a pretty good book about dealing with obsessive thoughts and struggling with the guilt that ultimately destroys.
    a. fact
    b. opinion
    c. combination of fact and opinion

____6. Government is, by nature, always wasteful and inefficient.
    a. fact
    b. opinion
    c. combination of fact and opinion

B. Directions: Read the following paragraph and answer the questions that follow.

[1]The composer Irving Berlin lived from 1888-1989 and could not read a note of music. [2]However, he compiled perhaps the largest repertoire of any twentieth-century songwriter. [3]All of his songs express simple, honest, and universal emotions. [4]While Berlin could define the everlasting joys of love, he was at his best when providing the bittersweet happiness of nostalgia. "I'm Dreaming of a White Christmas" is one of his most memorable songs. [5]This and other songs of the period were treasured by millions who could listen to the words, close their eyes, and relive their past.

—Adapted from Janaro and Altshuler, *The Art of Being Human,* 8th ed., p. 230.

_____7. Sentence 1 is an example of _____.
   a. fact
   b. opinion
   c. combination of fact and opinion

_____8. A biased word in sentence 3 is _____.
   a. songs
   b. honest
   c. universal
   d. emotions

_____9. Sentence 3 is an example of _____.
   a. fact
   b. opinion
   c. combination of fact and opinion

_____10. A biased word in sentence 4 is _____.
   a. define
   b. love
   c. best
   d. providing

124

Name_____ Section _____ Date _____ Score (number correct) _____ x 10 = _____

A. Directions: Read the statements and decide if they are facts, opinions, or a combination of fact and opinion

_____1. The government should reduce the growth of Medicare spending.
     a. fact
     b. opinion
     c. combination of fact and opinion

_____2. Many public schools do not offer information about birth control.
     a. fact
     b. opinion
     c. combination of fact and opinion

_____3. Because of the Monica Lewinsky affair, President Clinton was considered one of the most immoral presidents of the 20th century.
     a. fact
     b. opinion
     c. combination of fact and opinion

_____4. President Bush is the 43rd president of the United States, but there have been only 42 presidents.
     a. fact
     b. opinion
     c. combination of fact and opinion

_____5. The size of the universe is mind-boggling; the sun is only one of the more than 200 billion stars in our galaxy, the Milky Way, and the Milky Way is one of billions of galaxies in the universe.
     a. fact
     b. opinion
     c. combination of fact and opinion

_____6. Mecca is a city in Saudi Arabia with 618,000 inhabitants; Mecca is located about 80 kilometers from the Red Sea coast and is built around a natural well.
     a. fact
     b. opinion
     c. combination of fact and opinion

B. Directions: Read the following paragraph and answer the questions that follow.

[1]College student gambling appears to be on the rise on college campuses across the nation. [2]It was reported that in 2005, 15.5 percent of college students reported gambling once a week, up from 8.3 percent in 2002, an 87 percent increase. [3]College students have easier access to gambling opportunities than ever before with the advent of online gambling. [4]Many young people are spending an unhealthy amount of time and money participating in online poker tournaments. [5]Whereas casual gamblers can stop anytime they wish and are capable of seeing the necessity to do so, compulsive gamblers are unable to control the urge to gamble even in the face of devastating consequences: high debt, legal problems, and the loss of everything meaningful.

—Adapted from Donatelle, *Access to Health*, 10th ed., p. 355.

_____7. A biased word in sentence 1 is _____.
   a. gambling
   b. appears
   c. rise
   d. college

_____8. Sentence 2 is an example of _____.
   a. fact
   b. opinion
   c. combination of fact and opinion

_____9. Sentence 3 is an example of _____.
   a. fact
   b. opinion
   c. combination of fact and opinion

_____10. A biased word in sentence 5 is _____.
   a. gamblers
   b. unable
   c. wish
   d. devastating

126

Name_____ Section _____ Date _____ Score (number correct) _____ x 10 = _____

Directions: Read the following paragraph and answer the questions that follow.

[1]A pioneer work in American opera was composed in 1911 by Scott Joplin (1868–1917), famous for his innovations in ragtime. [2]Titled *Tremonisha*, it was the first major opera by an African American, and in 1911 it was snubbed by the opera establishment. [3]Joplin, already a success because of his ragtime achievements, had to publish the work himself. [4]In 1915 it was finally produced and received generally unfavorable notices.

—Janaro & Altshuler, *The Art of Being Human,* 7th ed., p. 301.

_____1.   Sentence 1 is an example of _____.
      a.   fact
      b.   opinion
      c.   combination of fact and opinion

_____2.   Sentence 2 is an example of _____.
      a.   fact
      b.   opinion
      c.   combination of fact and opinion

_____3.   Sentence 3 is an example of _____.
      a.   fact
      b.   opinion
      c.   combination of fact and opinion

_____4.   Sentence 4 is an example of _____.
      a.   fact
      b.   opinion
      c.   combination of fact and opinion

[1]Two possible reasons come to mind to explain the opera's failure. [2]One may be that the opera world, almost exclusively a white institution, resented Joplin's effort to create grand opera rather than continue producing music "appropriate" for his cultural heritage. [3]Another may be that audiences who knew and loved Joplin's music were expecting a ragtime opera, but Joplin wanted to go lightly in his use of the tempo that had served him so well. [4]Although there is some ragtime, he may have wanted to show that music transcended narrow racial ties.

—Janaro & Altshuler, *The Art of Being Human,* 7th ed., pp. 301–302.

_____5.   Sentence 2 is an example of _____.
      a.   fact
      b.   opinion
      c.   combination of fact and opinion

_____6. Sentence 3 is an example of _____.
      a. fact
      b. opinion
      c. combination of fact and opinion

_____7. Sentence 4 is an example of _____.
      a. fact
      b. opinion
      c. combination of fact and opinion

[1]As happens over and over in the history of humanities, time has reversed the original criticism. [2]*Tremonisha* is now widely accepted as the first truly American opera, using American subject matter and American folk themes along with a symphonic score inspired by Wagner's music. [3]Although Joplin did in fact admire Wagner above all composers and even followed in the German composer's footsteps by writing both libretto and music, the result has been a recognized masterpiece in the romantic tradition that combines traditional forms with American motifs.

_____8. Sentence 1 is an example of _____.
      a. fact
      b. opinion
      c. combination of fact and opinion

_____9. Sentence 2 is an example of _____.
      a. fact
      b. opinion
      c. combination of fact and opinion

_____10. Sentence 3 is an example of _____.
      a. fact
      b. opinion
      c. combination of fact and opinion

CHAPTER 9: FACT AND OPINION
Lab 9.5 MASTERY TEST 1

Name_____ Section _____ Date _____ Score (number correct) _____ x 10 = _____

A. Directions: Read the statements and decide if they are facts, opinions, or a combination of fact and opinion

_____1. When he was two years old, Tiger Woods appeared on *CBS News* and *The Mike Douglas Show* putting with Bob Hope.
    a. fact
    b. opinion
    c. combination of fact and opinion

_____2. The U.S. Mint buys strips of metal about 13 inches wide and 1,500 feet long to manufacture the nickel, dime, quarter, half-dollar, and dollar.
    a. fact
    b. opinion
    c. combination of fact and opinion

_____3. Tupac Shakur was one of the most influential rappers ever; his lyrics, actions, and offstage antics outraged people all over the world.
    a. fact
    b. opinion
    c. combination of fact and opinion

_____4. Afeni Shakur, Tupac's mother, spent time in prison while she was pregnant with Tupac.
    a. fact
    b. opinion
    c. combination of fact and opinion

_____5. On a physical level, yoga postures, called *asanas*, are designed to tone, strengthen, and align the body.
    a. fact
    b. opinion
    c. combination of fact and opinion

_____6. On the mental level, yoga uses breathing techniques and meditation to quiet, clarify, and discipline the mind.
    a. fact
    b. opinion
    c. combination of fact and opinion

B. Directions: Read the following paragraph and answer the questions that follow.

[1]Most of us are aware that sometimes our first impressions and reasons for being attracted to another are not completely rational. [2]Sudden lust, love at first sight, or the intense dislike of someone with whom we have had no previous contact can seem inexplicable. [3]Many social psychologists suggest that relationship development has a lot to do with "chemistry" between the individuals in the relationship. [4]The chemistry explanation probably holds some truth, but many other variables influence the development of a relationship.

—Adapted from Seiler and Beall, *Communication: Making Connections*. 7th ed., p. 385.

_____7. Sentence 1 is an example of _____.
      a. fact
      b. opinion
      c. combination of fact and opinion

_____8. A biased word in sentence 2 is _____.
      a. first
      b. dislike
      c. previous
      d. seem

_____9. Sentence 3 is an example of _____.
      a. fact
      b. opinion
      c. combination of fact and opinion

_____10. A biased word in sentence 4 is _____.
      a. explanation
      b. probably
      c. variables
      d. influence

Name_____Section _____ Date _____ Score (number correct) _____ x 10 = _____

Objective: To identify an author's use of facts and opinions in reading passages.

A. Directions: Read the statements and decide if they are facts, opinions, or a combination of fact and opinion.

_____1. The novel *Huckleberry Finn* by Mark Twain should be banned from required reading lists in public schools.
    a. fact
    b. opinion
    c. combination of fact and opinion

_____2. Chiropractors believe that if our spines are healthy, we will feel better and enjoy life more.
    a. fact
    b. opinion
    c. combination of fact and opinion

_____3. Many of the first modern chiropractors were jailed for practicing medicine without a license.
    a. fact
    b. opinion
    c. combination of fact and opinion

_____4. In 1944, the G.I. Bill paid for veterans to study chiropractic after they left the service.
    a. fact
    b. opinion
    c. combination of fact and opinion

_____5. A loving husband should know what his wife's emotional needs are without being told.
    a. fact
    b. opinion
    c. combination of fact and opinion

_____6. Drug use among adolescents has decreased during the past five years.
    a. fact
    b. opinion
    c. combination of fact and opinion

B. Directions: Read the following paragraph and answer the questions that follow.

[1]On April 18, 1946, the sports world focused on a baseball field in Jersey City, New Jersey, an industrial wasteland on the banks of the Passaic River. [2]It was the opening day for the Jersey City Giants of the International League. [3]Their opponents were the Montreal Royals. [4]Playing second base for the Royals was Jackie Roosevelt Robinson. [5]He was a pigeon-toed, highly competitive, marvelously talented African American athlete. [6]The stadium was filled with curious, excited spectators, and in the press box, sportswriters from all over fidgeted with their typewriters. [7]It was not just another season-opening game. [8]Professional baseball, America's national game, was about to be integrated.

—Martin et al., *America and Its People: A Mosaic in the Making,* 3rd ed., p. 948.

_____7. Sentence 1 is an example of _____.
- a. fact
- b. opinion
- c. combination of fact and opinion

_____8. A biased word in sentence 1 is _____.
- a. sports world
- b. baseball
- c. industrial
- d. wasteland

_____9. Sentence 4 is an example of _____.
- a. fact
- b. opinion
- c. combination of fact and opinion

_____10. A biased word in sentence 5 is _____.
- a. pigeon-toed
- b. marvelously
- c. African American
- d. athlete

132

Name_____ Section _____ Date _____ Score (number correct) _____ x 10 = _____

Objective: To identify the author's tone and purpose.
Directions: Choose the word that best expresses the writer's tone in the passage.

Alonzo winked at his mother's shocked gaze and with a grin quipped, "Sausage and pepperoni pizza for breakfast makes perfect sense. Allow me to demonstrate. You have your tomato. Tomato is technically a fruit. You have your cheese. Cheese is a dairy product. You have your crust—necessary carbs for quick energy in the morning. And don't forget the sausage and pepperoni—my protein. If you think about it, it's just like bacon and eggs, toast, and orange juice." Still grinning, he added, "Really it is. Well, almost. Why are you looking at me that way?"

_____1. The primary purpose of this passage is _____.
        a.   to entertain
        b.   to inform
        c.   to persuade

_____2. The tone of this passage is _____.
        a.   humorous
        b.   ironic
        c.   sad
        d.   factual

Do you want to add years to your life and feel better too? Here are a few tips. First, to decrease your chances of a heart attack, eat a handful of nuts each day. Also, to ease the effects of rheumatoid arthritis, be sure to include some citrus, such as orange juice, in your diet. Finally, exercise on a regular basis. Include weight-bearing activities such as walking and jogging. Also, try yoga for flexibility and stress relief.

_____3. The primary purpose of this passage is _____.
        a.   to entertain
        b.   to inform
        c.   to persuade

_____4. The tone of this passage is _____.
        a.   insulting
        b.   encouraging
        c.   demanding
        d.   exasperated

Circadian rhythms have fascinated scientists for many years. Recognizing that the eye nerves translate information to the brain about the time of day, scientists observe that we adapt to the conditions around us. Also, these researchers have recently discovered that not everyone is alike. For example, teenagers are nocturnal. That is, they are more active at night but do not function as well early in the morning.

133

_____5. The primary purpose of this passage is _____.
     a. to entertain
     b. to inform
     c. to persuade

_____6. The tone of this passage is _____.
     a. approving
     b. demanding
     c. sarcastic
     d. objective

Because researchers studying circadian rhythms have discovered that most teenagers are really nocturnal, school administrators should take this into account when organizing a school day. For example, traditionally teenagers must arise in the predawn hours and arrive at school before sunrise. Groggy and unfocused, they find it difficult to concentrate and be alert before lunch. After lunch, which for many students in overcrowded high schools begins at 10:30 a.m., they are finally able to pay attention. Armed with this information, the school board should be innovative and rearrange the schedule, which would curb truancy in grades 8 through 12.

_____7. The primary purpose of this passage is _____.
     a. to entertain
     b. to inform
     c. to persuade

_____8. The tone of this passage is _____.
     a. informative
     b. cynical
     c. bossy
     d. outraged

One of the creators of Cranium, Richard Tait, a former Microsoft executive, said he wanted to invent a game that allowed people to leave the board feeling good. He wanted a game that involved chance as well as skill, one in which people could have fun together and not feel so competitive. Four people or several teams can play one of today's hottest-selling games, Cranium. While some moves on the game board may require that a team member know the name of the largest mammal on earth (the blue whale), other moves may ask participants to hum songs, pantomime people, or spell words backward. At the end, though, all the teams feel good because they have had so much fun. Every household should purchase Cranium. You will discover it is better than TV. Also, it will stimulate your brain and encourage people to have fun together.

_____9. The primary purpose of this passage is _____.
     a. to entertain
     b. to inform
     c. to persuade

_____10. The tone of this passage is _____.
     a. accusing
     b. positive
     c. amused
     d. argumentative

Name_____ Section _____ Date _____ Score (number correct) _____ x 10 = _____

Objective: To identify the author's tone and purpose.

Directions: Read the paragraphs and answer the questions that follow.

The moment the words were out of my mouth, I wished I could take them back. I didn't mean to hurt Ted's feelings. He is such a nice person, and he certainly doesn't deserve to be treated so poorly. I guess the stress from my job has been more than I can handle. Instead of taking my problems out on him, I need to deal directly with the people who create the stress. If only I didn't care so much what people thought of me at work, then maybe it would be easier to confront them. This much I know, however: I don't ever want to hurt Ted like that again.

_____1. The tone of this paragraph can be described as _____.
      a. objective
      b. regretful
      c. admiring
      d. hateful

_____2. The primary purpose of this paragraph is to _____.
      a. persuade
      b. entertain
      c. inform

In his now-classic political treatise *Leviathan* (1651), Hobbes argued pessimistically that man's natural state was war. Government, Hobbes theorized, particularly a monarchy, was necessary to restrain man's bestial tendencies because life without government was a "state of nature."

—O'Connor & Sabato, *The Essentials of American Government*, p. 16.

_____3. According to the passage, Hobbes's tone could be described as _____.
      a. critical
      b. amused
      c. playful
      d. confused

_____4. The primary purpose of this paragraph is to _____.
      a. persuade
      b. entertain
      c. inform

British-born Alfred Hitchcock (1899–1980) was imported to make scary melodramas and only gradually acquired the <u>critical reputation</u> his work continues to <u>merit</u>. Known first as a man who made thrillers about spies and murders among highly civilized people, he was dubbed the "<u>master of suspense</u>" in the late 1930s. The plots of his films were filled with unexpected twists of danger, as in the 1942 spy film *Saboteur,* when hero and villain have their showdown fight to the death on the torch of the Statue of Liberty.

—Janaro & Altshuler, *The Art of Being Human,* 6th ed., p. 348.

_____5. The underlined words indicate a tone of _____
     a. sentimentality
     b. irreverence
     c. scolding
     d. admiration

_____6. The primary purpose of this paragraph is to _____ .
     a. persuade
     b. entertain
     c. inform

"Evil," observed Hitchcock once in an interview, "is complete disorder." That his villains were overcome in the end is the price he had to pay to Hollywood's moral code. Yet his so-called happy endings are often injected with sly humor, as if to say, "The world really isn't so well run." He believed implicitly that we live in a fundamentally amoral universe in which good triumphs only by accident, in which good is a human intervention practiced successfully by a few whose survival is by no means sure, and in which chaos is the law of nature itself.

—Janaro & Altshuler, *The Art of Being Human,* 6th ed., p. 348.

_____7. The tone of this passage is _____ .
     a. calm
     b. cheerful
     c. cynical
     d. encouraging

_____8. The primary purpose of this paragraph is to _____ .
     a. persuade
     b. entertain
     c. inform

Alfred Hitchcock was a product of British society that was outwardly civilized but had fostered Jack the Ripper, a serial killer from a genteel background, as well as many other gory crimes. Hitchcock combined a civilized directing style with a zest for the bizarre and frightening. The real oddity, of course, is that he was a film director who believed that disorder and chaos were fundamental to both human nature and the natural world, yet who communicated his belief in a very planned, meticulously offered way. He put down in writing the intricate details of each shot before the camera was ever turned on.

—Adapted from Janaro & Altshuler, *The Art of Being Human*, 6th ed., p. 350.

____9. The tone of this passage is _____.
      a. demanding
      b. approving
      c. ironic
      d. insulting

____10. The primary purpose of this paragraph is to _____.
      a. persuade
      b. entertain
      c. inform

Name_____ Section _____ Date _____ Score (number correct) _____ x 10 = _____

A. Directions: Read the paragraphs and answer the questions that follow.

Racial prejudice is a sin against humanity. How does one dare to think less of another human being simply because of color or ethnic origin? How does one dare to think of oneself as so much more special or righteous than another? To do so is the height of arrogance. And those who sit in silence as discrimination takes place are no better than those who discriminate. Those who sit in silence and listen to words of hate are no better than those who speak those very words. Shame on those whose love of their own color drives them to hate those of different hues. Shame on those whose love of their own voices drowns out the rich tones of diversity. Shame on those of us who let them.

____1. The primary purpose of this paragraph is _____.
    a. to entertain
    b. to inform
    c. to persuade

____2. The tone of this passage is _____.
    a. flattering
    b. approving
    c. sarcastic
    d. outraged

While few equate immorality with criminality, the similarities are striking. First, moral codes and laws are linguistically expressed, often employing words such as *shall* and *shall not*. Second, at the heart of both concepts is the idea of intentionality, meaning that it is reasonable to hold people both morally and legally responsible for behavior that they intended to happen. Third, most believe that it is appropriate to punish people who violate both moral codes and criminal statutes, unless those people happen to be very young. Finally, there is considerable overlap between the acts that are considered criminal [and those considered immoral].

—Ellis & Walsh, *Criminology,* pp. 313–14.

____3. The tone of this paragraph can be described as _____.
    a. emotional
    b. neutral
    c. disbelieving
    d. ironic

____4. The primary purpose of this paragraph is to _____.
    a. persuade
    b. entertain
    c. inform

Renewed

The afternoon finds me, on the front porch in the same rocker
mother used to quiet our baby fears, searching for peace.
The steady plop of rain drops on the mulch in the azalea beds,
the fresh, sweet scent of the newly washed earth,
the glistening greens of grass, and trees, and shrubs,
the steamy mist rising from the black top road,
All awaken me to a moment created by Hands
stronger and more sure than mine.
And peace comes to me.

—Unknown

_____5. The purpose of this poem is _____.
     a. to entertain the reader with personal thoughts about the soothing effects of nature
     b. to persuade the reader to protect the environment
     c. to inform the reader about facts related to nature

B. Directions: Read this passage and answer the questions that follow.

How Relationships End

[1]A declining relationship usually follows one of several paths. [2]Sometimes a relationship loses steam and runs down like a dying battery. Instead of a single event that causes the breakup, the relationship **fades away**—the two partners just drift further and further apart. [3]They spend less time together, let more time go by before seeing each other again. [4]You've probably had a number of friendships that ended this way—perhaps long-distance relationships. [5]Long-distance relationships require a great deal of effort to maintain, so a move can easily decrease the level of intimacy.

[6]Some relationships end in sudden death. [7]As the name suggests, **sudden death** moves straight to separation. [8]One partner might move away or die, or more frequently, a single event such as infidelity, breaking a confidence, a major conflict, or some other major violation precipitates the breakup. [9]Sudden death is like taking an express elevator from a top floor to ground level.

[10]In between fading away and sudden death lies incrementalism. [11]**Incrementalism** is the process by which conflicts and problems continue to accumulate in the relationship until they reach a critical mass that leads to the breakup; the relationship becomes intolerable or, from a social exchange perspective, too costly. [12]"I just got to a point where it wasn't worth it anymore," and "It got to the point where all we did was fight all the time," are typical statements about incremental endings.

—Beebe, Beebe, & Redmond, _Interpersonal Communication,_ 3rd ed., pp. 344–45.

_____6. The topic of the passage is _____.
     a. the sudden death of a relationship
     b. the paths declining relationships take as they end
     c. incrementalism
     d. what makes a good relationship

_____7. The central idea of the passage is expressed in which sentence?
      a.   sentence 1
      b.   sentence 2
      c.   sentence 6
      d.   sentence 11

_____8. The word *perspective* as it is used in sentence 11 means _____.
      a.   discussion
      b.   view
      c.   exchange
      d.   translation

_____9. The purpose of this passage is
      a.   to inform the reader of the paths declining relationships take.
      b.   to persuade the reader not to get entangled in a new relationship.
      c.   to entertain the reader with relationship failure stories.
      d.   to persuade the reader of ways to avoid a declining relationship.

_____10. "I just got to a point where it wasn't worth it anymore" and "It got to the point where all we did was fight all the time." What is the tone of these comments from paragraph 3?
      a.   bias
      b.   relief
      c.   joy
      d.   exasperation

Name_____ Section _____ Date _____ Score (number correct) _____ x 10 = _____

Directions: Choose the word that best expresses the writer's tone in the passage.

In naval aviation, the AWACS (Airborne Early Warning Command and Control System) plane, or Hawkeye, serves as an air traffic controller, monitoring the airspace around a carrier fleet. It is responsible for surveillance of enemy aircraft and ships as well as directing helicopters to survivors and guarding against air collisions. In addition to servicing the Navy, Hawkeye planes have been used in rescue operations of civilians during hurricane evacuations.

_____1. The primary purpose of this passage is _____.
     a. to entertain
     b. to inform
     c. to persuade

_____2. The tone of this passage is _____.
     a. humorous
     b. ironic
     c. confident
     d. factual

The pilots of the Hawkeye aircraft are the unsung heroes of naval operations. The first in and the last out, these men receive none of the glory bestowed on the Top Guns of F-18 fame. Thanks to Hollywood, fighter pilots have been glorified, but the pilots of the AWACS planes work quietly and diligently, and they deserve praise for their contributions.

_____3. The primary purpose of this passage is _____.
     a. to entertain
     b. to inform
     c. to persuade

_____4. The tone of this passage is _____.
     a. admiring
     b. ironic
     c. unbiased
     d. humorous

Tobacco companies have been in litigation, facing charges that their marketing practices in the past have targeted teenagers. Also, evidence indicates that companies adjusted levels of nicotine in their cigarettes to increase the probability that smokers would become addicted to the product to ensure higher sales in the future.

_____5. The primary purpose of this passage is _____.
     a. to entertain
     b. to inform
     c. to persuade

141

_____6. The tone of this passage is _____.
      a. horrified
      b. bitter
      c. regretful
      d. objective

Tobacco companies should be forced to pay lucrative settlements to anyone who has become addicted or adversely affected by the use of their products. Anyone who has a loved one who has succumbed to the temptation to use cigarettes can attest to the way the product can swallow souls as well as consumers' wallets. The clinical evidence of the devastation created by secondhand smoke is compelling enough for legislators to consider legal action against the powerful corporations. Unfortunately, tobacco companies have traditionally provided strong financial support for many political candidates. Write your congressional representative and express your outrage!

_____7. The primary purpose of this passage is _____.
      a. to entertain
      b. to inform
      c. to persuade

_____8. The tone of this passage is _____.
      a. outraged
      b. sad
      c. surprised
      d. confused

Game night at our house was hilarious when we played Cranium with two teams of three. Imagine Abram, the savvy surfer, doing an impression of Marilyn Monroe singing "Happy Birthday." Or Dave, the macho bodybuilder, swinging his hips and singing a medley of Madonna's songs. But the most memorable was George's Cranium Doodle hint for the architectural term "flying buttress." It was, well, side-splittingly outrageous!

_____9. The primary purpose of this passage is _____.
      a. to entertain
      b. to inform
      c. to persuade

_____10. The tone of this passage is _____.
      a. accusing
      b. lively
      c. critical
      d. argumentative

Name_____ Section _____ Date _____ Score (number correct) _____ x 10 = _____

A. Directions: Read the paragraphs and answer the questions that follow.

Students who cheat are losers who cause more damage than they know. First of all, cheaters hurt others. Cheaters can end up with higher grade-point averages, which makes them unfairly eligible for recommendations, awards, and scholarships that they don't deserve. By cheating, they rob hardworking students of their fair chance. Second, cheaters hurt the schools from which they graduate. They carry their lack of real skills with them into the job force. Their ineptness reflects poorly on the college or university that trained them. Finally, cheaters cheat themselves. They lose out on attaining real skills and knowledge that will serve them the rest of their lives. So while cheaters may think they are really smart and beating the system, they are the real losers.

_____1. The primary purpose of this paragraph is to _____.
     a. persuade
     b. entertain
     c. inform

_____2. The tone of this paragraph can be described as _____.
     a. critical
     b. regretful
     c. ironic
     d. sympathetic

Makinsey's breath caught short in her throat at the sound of the twig's snap. She could hear something panting in the bushes nearby, but the night beyond the campfire was too black to see anything. The hair on the back of her neck stood on end, and a network of needlelike pricks spread across her skin. She tried to shout "Mother," but no sound came out. The panting seemed to come closer. She whirled the trunk of her body around first to the left and then to the right as her eyes frantically searched the darkness. Nothing! *I need a weapon*, she thought. From the woodpile by her side, she chose a log that was as thick as her arm and felt balanced in her hand. She placed one end in the fire until it blazed to life. With the torch in hand, she turned to face the panting that was now much louder and much closer.

_____3. The primary purpose of this paragraph is to _____.
     a. persuade
     b. entertain
     c. inform

_____4. The tone of this paragraph can be described as _____.
     a. critical
     b. demanding
     c. fearful
     d. objective

Machine or artificial intelligence (AI) is a specialty area of computer science concerned with creating machines capable of functions that, in humans, require consciousness or intelligence. Whether or not there *can* be machine intelligence is a hotly debated point. We suggest that if intelligence can exist to varying degrees in living beings, then machine intelligence can exist even if it is no more than equivalent to the minimal living form. Let's just be reasonable and realistic in our expectations—perhaps even suspend disbelief—and we may be rewarded for our flexibility.

—Lockard & Abrams, *Computers for Twenty-First Century Educators,* p. 287.

____5. The tone in this introductory paragraph to a technology textbook is _____.
- a. sorrowful and disappointed
- b. critical and arrogant
- c. informative and pessimistic
- d. informative and optimistic

____6. The primary purpose of this paragraph is to _____.
- a. persuade
- b. entertain
- c. inform

B. Directions: Read the passage, which is the foreword to *A Night to Remember* by Walter Lord, and then answer the questions that follow it.

[1]In 1898 a struggling author named Morgan Robertson concocted a novel about a fabulous Atlantic liner, far larger than any that had ever been built. [2]Robertson loaded his ship with rich and complacent people and then wrecked it one cold April night on an iceberg. [3]This somehow showed the futility of everything, and, in fact, the book was called *Futility* when it appeared that year, published by the firm of M. F. Mansfield.

[4]Fourteen years later a British shipping company named the White Star Line built a steamer remarkably like the one in Robertson's novel. [5]The new liner was 66,000 tons displacement; Robertson's was 70,000. [6]The real ship was 882.5 feet long; the fictional one was 800 feet. [7]Both vessels were triple screw and could make 24–25 knots. [8]Both could carry about 3,000 people, and both had enough lifeboats for only a fraction of this number. [9]But, then, this didn't seem to matter because both were labeled "unsinkable."

[10]On April 10, 1912, the real ship left Southampton on her maiden voyage to New York. [11]Her cargo included a priceless copy of the Rubáiyát of Omar Khayyám and a list of passengers collectively worth two hundred fifty million dollars. [12]On her way over she too struck an iceberg and went down on a cold April night.

[13]Robertson called his ship the *Titan*; the White Star Line called its ship the *Titanic.*

144

_____7. The topic of the passage is

      a. odd occurrences in history and why people should pay attention to details.

      b. true stories in naval history that have some amazing outcomes and can be predicted by civilians.

      c. the disaster of the _Titanic_ and things the engineers could have done to prevent it.

      d. the similarity in the earlier fictional account of the _Titan_ and the later real story of the _Titanic._

_____8. The purpose of the passage is _____.

      a. to inform.

      b. to persuade.

      c. to entertain

_____9. Which word describes the tone in sentence 1?

      a. gloomy

      b. factual

      c. admiring

      d. unbiased

_____10. Which word describes the tone in sentences 6-8?

      a. jovial

      b. flippant

      c. objective

      d. biased

Name_____ Section _____ Date _____ Score (number correct) _____ x 10 = _____

Directions: Read the paragraphs and answer the questions that follow

Dr. Martin Luther King, Jr., was one of those rare men who fulfilled his destiny. There can be little doubt that he lived a life based on the principles of courage and sacrifice. There can be no argument that his courage and sacrifice have instilled those principles in others. He was a man who would not allow the limited views of the small-minded to define his world or direct his steps. He was a man who faced death unflinchingly so that others could live lives of which he could only dream. King was indeed a king among men.

_____1. The primary purpose of this paragraph is to _____.
     a. persuade
     b. entertain
     c. inform

_____2. The tone of this paragraph can be described as _____.
     a. critical
     b. regretful
     c. ironic
     d. admiring

Many people who begin exercise programs do so without proper preparation. This lack of preparation can lead to serious injuries. A few simple steps can help avoid these unnecessary injuries. Before the workout, stretch. Taking a few minutes to stretch warms up the muscles and prevents strains and tears. During the workout, drink plenty of water. A good workout causes a loss of body fluids through sweating. Staying hydrated ensures that muscles can perform properly. After the workout, stretch again. Stretching after the workout reduces muscle tension and improves circulation. In addition, stretching an already warmed-up muscle encourages greater range in mobility and flexibility.

_____3. The primary purpose of this paragraph is to _____.
     a. persuade
     b. entertain
     c. inform

_____4. The tone of this paragraph can be described as _____.
     a. critical
     b. demanding
     c. fearful
     d. objective

It is unlikely that human nature will suddenly change drastically—that we will abruptly lose our environmental manipulativeness. What we must seek instead are ways to be more accommodating with other species and with the biosphere. Those of us living in affluent developed nations are responsible for the greatest amount of environmental degradation. Our long-term welfare and that of future generations demand that we work toward changing some of our values, learning to revere the natural processes that sustain us and reducing our orientation toward short-term personal gain. The current state of the biosphere demonstrates that we are treading precariously on uncharted ecological ground. The importance of our scientific and personal efforts cannot be overstated.

—Campbell, Reece, Taylor, and Simon, *Biology: Concepts & Connections*, 5th ed., 781.

_____ 5. The primary purpose of this paragraph is to _____.
      a. persuade
      b. entertain
      c. inform

_____ 6. The tone of this paragraph can be described as _____.
      a. serious
      b. humorous
      c. fearful
      d. disbelieving

[1]The suicide rate increases over the lifespan, from childhood to old age, but it jumps sharply at adolescence. [2]Currently, suicide is the third-leading cause of death (after motor vehicle collisions and homicides) among American youths and the second-leading cause (after motor vehicle collisions) among Canadian youths. [3]Perhaps because North American teenagers experience more stress and fewer supports than in the past, the adolescent suicide rate tripled in both the United States and Canada between the mid-1960s and the mid-1990s.

[4]Despite girls' higher rates of depression, the number of boys who kill themselves exceeds the number of girls by a ratio of 4 or 5 to 1. [5]Girls make more unsuccessful suicide attempts, using methods from which they are more likely to be revived, such as a sleeping pill overdose. [6]In contrast, boys tend to choose techniques that lead to instant death, such as firearms or hanging. [7]Gender-role expectations may be responsible; less tolerance exists for feelings of helplessness and failed efforts in males than in females. [8]Many depressed young people conclude that no one could possibly understand their intense pain, and their despair and hopelessness deepen.

[9]To prevent suicides, parents and teachers must be trained to pick up on the signals that a troubled teenager sends. [10] Schools, recreation, and religious organizations must all be equipped to provide sympathetic counselors, peer support groups, and telephone hot lines. [11]A watchful eye must be kept on vulnerable adolescents. [12]We must all do our part.

—Donatelle, *Access to Health*, 10th ed., p. 420.

_____ 7. The topic of the passage is _____.
      a. differences between suicide attempts between boys and girls
      b. stories of adolescent suicide attempts
      c. the dangers of gender-role expectations
      d. the increasing adolescent suicide rate

_____8. The purpose of the first two paragraphs is _____.
- a. to inform
- b. to persuade
- c. to entertain

_____9. The purpose of the last paragraph is _____.
- a. to inform
- b. to persuade
- c. to entertain

_____10. The overall tone of this passage is _____.
- a. concerned
- b. bitter
- c. admiring
- d. argumentative

Name_____ Section _____ Date _____ Score (number correct) _____ x 10 = _____

Objective: To use supporting details to make accurate inferences.

Directions: Read the passage below. Decide if the following statements are valid inferences that are firmly based on the information in the passage.

In 1999, the world's population surpassed 6 billion. Ninety-seven percent of each year's population growth occurs in the poorest parts of the world. Experts believe that by 2050, the world population will grow to over 9 billion. Many scientists think that overpopulation has caused a loss of large areas of forest and topsoil. Some also believe that uncontrolled population growth will lead to worldwide shortages of food and energy. For the past half century, people concerned about overpopulation have called for population control. The following statistics are based on current population:

- 300 million women want family planning but do not have information about it or the means to get it.
- 1 billion people have no access to health care.
- 1.3 billion people live in poverty.
- 840 million people don't have enough food to stay healthy.
- 85 countries do not have the ability to grow or buy enough food to feed their citizens.
- 1.5 billion people do not have access to safe drinking water.

—Adapted from Donatelle, *Health: The Basics*, 5th ed., p. 406.

_____1. The world will not be able to feed its population by 2050.
     a. valid inference
     b. not a valid inference

_____2. Poor people should not have children.
     a. valid inference
     b. not a valid inference

_____3. Poor people are more likely to have many children.
     a. valid inference
     b. not a valid inference

_____4. Many people are outraged by overpopulation.
     a. valid inference
     b. not a valid inference

_____5. Some people fear the effects of overpopulation.
     a. valid inference
     b. not a valid inference

_____6. The world is overpopulated.
   a.   valid inference
   b.   not a valid inference

_____7. Some people want to limit the number of children people have.
   a.   valid inference
   b.   not a valid inference

_____8. The statistics are likely to rise in the upcoming years.
   a.   valid inference
   b.   not a valid inference

_____9. Overpopulation is the main cause of starvation
   a.   valid inference
   b.   not a valid inference

_____10. About twenty percent of the population lives in poverty.
   a.   valid inference
   b.   not a valid inference

Name_____ Section _____ Date _____ Score (number correct) _____ x 10 = _____

Objective: To use supporting details to make accurate inferences.

A. Directions: Read the sentence below. Decide if the following statements are valid inferences that are firmly based on the information in the sentence.

Posted on the wall beside the elevators and above an ashtray full of cigarette butts is a sign stating, "This is NOT a smoking area."

_____1. People are smoking in a nonsmoking area.
     a.   valid inference
     b.   not a valid inference

_____2. Authorities provided the ashtray because they expect people to ignore the NO SMOKING sign.
     a.   valid inference
     b.   not a valid inference

_____3. The ashtray is offered so that people can obey the sign.
     a.   valid inference
     b.   not a valid inference

B. Directions: Read each of the following groups of sentences, and then select the letter of the accurate inference based on the details presented.

- The thermostat always reads below 65 degrees in Chris's home.
- Each evening a fire blazes in the fireplace.
- Frequently, candles of varying sizes flicker in the den and kitchen.

_____4. What can you infer from these details?
     a.   The power is out.
     b.   Chris does not care if the other family members are uncomfortable.
     c.   Chris prefers cool temperatures and the illumination of candles and a fire.
     d.   Chris will soon be sick from the cooler temperatures in his home.

- The sign reads, "First Time Ever Sale! Omni Game Box Now Half Off!"
- A line of patrons snakes along the aisle by the customer-service counter.
- Each patron has a sales receipt in one hand and an Omni Game Box in the other.

_____5. What can you infer from these details?
     a.   Customers who bought the Omni Game Box are displeased with their purchase.
     b.   Omni Game Box is a poorly made imitation of a good product.
     c.   Customers want to exchange their Omni Game Boxes for a better product.
     d.   Customers want to return their Omni Game Boxes.

151

- Dandelions and buttercups dot the field.
- Sweater-clad families spread the contents of their picnic baskets on blankets.
- Some children are flying kites in the blustery wind.

_____6. What can you infer from these details?
    a.   It is fall, and a hurricane warning has been issued.
    b.   It is the Fourth of July.
    c.   The season is spring.
    d.   It is a Sunday afternoon in the park.

- A sprinkler whirrs over a green lawn, which sports a sign saying, "Well water used here."
- Next door, the grass is sparse, and the shrubs and flowers are brown and wilted.
- The cars in both driveways are covered with a film of dust.

_____7. What can you infer from these details?
    a.   The neighbors with the dying shrubs do not have a well.
    b.   There is a drought in the area, and watering restrictions are in effect.
    c.   The neighbor with the wilted flowers does not care about the landscape of the property.
    d.   The neighbor with the dying lawn and shrubs has not watered the lawn and garden enough.

C. Directions: Read the paragraphs and answer the questions that follow.

Stress is the mental and physical response of our bodies to the changes and challenges in our lives. A **stressor** is any physical, social, or psychological event or condition that causes the body to have to adjust to a specific situation. Stressors may be **tangible,** such as an angry parent, or intangible, such as the mixed emotions associated with meeting your significant other's parents for the first time. **Adjustment** is the attempt to cope with a given situation. During adjustment to a stressor, strain may develop. **Strain** is the wear and tear the body and mind sustain during the process of adjusting to or resisting a stressor.

—Adapted from Donatelle, *Access to Health,* pp. 64–65.

_____8. What can you infer from the information in this paragraph?
    a.   Stressors are usually not obvious.
    b.   A traffic jam is an example of an intangible stressor.
    c.   Fear of failure is an example of an intangible stressor.
    d.   Adjusting to or resisting a stressor is probably not possible.

In 1999, the world's population surpassed six billion. Ninety-seven percent of each year's population growth occurs in the poorest parts of the world. Experts believe that by 2050, the world population will grow to over nine billion. Many scientists think that overpopulation has caused a loss of large areas of forest and topsoil. Some also believe that uncontrolled population growth will lead to worldwide shortages of food and energy. For the past half century, people concerned about overpopulation have called for population control.

—Adapted from Donatelle, *Health: The Basics*, 5th ed., p. 406.

____9. What logical inference can you make from the information in this paragraph?
  a. Poor people should not have children.
  b. Many people are outraged by overpopulation.
  c. The statistics are likely to rise in the upcoming years.
  d. There will be a worldwide shortage of food and energy in 2050.

Each new class of college students represents a more savvy group of health consumers with its own unique perspectives on health. An astounding, often contradictory and confusing array of health information is available through the simple click of a mouse, the routine turning on of the television, cell phone, or other media device, or the casual perusal of a magazine. Because there is no one recipe for achieving health, it is important to consider the various opinions and options available to determine what information is the most scientifically defensible and which poses the least amount of risk to wellness.

—Adapted from Donatelle, *Access to Health,*, 10th ed., p. v.

____10. What logical inference can you make from the information in this paragraph?
  a. Sources on health issues sometimes state differing opinions.
  b. The Web is the most reliable source for health information.
  c. Choices about health care will never pose a risk to overall wellness.
  d. College students are more confused about health issues than ever before.

153

Name_____ Section _____ Date _____ Score (number correct) _____ x 10 = _____

A. Directions: Read the passage below. Decide if the following statements are valid inferences that are firmly based on the information in the passage.

Mara and Kimberly walked out to the parking lot at the same time. Each woman lugged identical sets of thick, heavy textbooks. Mara also struggled to hold on to the heavy jacket she had worn that morning. As Kimberly watched Mara battle with her coat and books, she was grateful she had grabbed only a sweater, which was now tied around her waist.

_____1. Mara and Kimberly are friends.
    a. valid inference
    b. not a valid inference

_____2. The weather warmed up during the day.
    a. valid inference
    b. not a valid inference

_____3. Mara and Kimberly take some of the same courses.
    a. valid inference
    b. not a valid inference

_____4. It is the summer season.
    a. valid inference
    b. not a valid inference

B. Directions: Read each of the following groups of sentences, and then select the letter of the accurate inference based on the details presented.

- All public restrooms in the town have the water faucets turned off and have hand sanitizers by the sink instead.
- In local public restaurants, food is served on paper plates and menus have handwritten notes, "Water will be served only on request."
- In local hotels, water fountains, which are turned off, have been replaced by containers of bottled water.

_____5. What can you infer from these details?
    a. The town is on water restrictions.
    b. The town's water supply has been contaminated.
    c. The local merchants are trying to save money by using less water.
    d. The cost of water has increased significantly in the area.

- The cottage deck railing is decorated with strings of colorful lights.
- Reggae music fills the air, and laughter ripples from the people inside, who are holding full Margarita glasses.
- The aroma of grilled blackened tuna wafts from the deck.

____ 6. What can you infer from these details?
  a. People are gathered for a birthday party.
  b. The occasion is a party after a wedding.
  c. It is Christmas at the beach.
  d. People have gathered to enjoy company, music, and food.

- The sky is pewter gray.
- The temperature has dropped rapidly and now hovers around 29 degrees.
- The humidity is 90 percent, and the barometric pressure is falling.

____ 7. What can you infer from these details?
  a. It will probably snow soon.
  b. The precipitation will begin as rain and taper off in a few hours.
  c. The precipitation will begin as snow and then change to rain.
  d. A hurricane is approaching.

- Rachel has cat figurines on the shelf by her bed.
- She wears a T-shirt that says, "Love me, love my cat."
- A box of kitty litter sits in the corner of the laundry room.

____ 8. What can you infer from these details?
  a. Rachel's cat has run away.
  b. Rachel is a cat lover.
  c. Rachel is obsessed with cats.
  d. Rachel loves cats but is allergic to them.

C. Directions: Read the following passage and answer the questions that follow.

Asian Americans were the fastest-growing minority group in the United States at the end of the 20th century. In 1999, there were nearly 11 million Americans of Asian or Pacific Island descent. Although they represented only 3.9 percent of the total U.S. population, they were increasing at seven times the national rate. Experts believe that by 2050, one in ten Americans will be of Asian origin.

Compared to other minorities, Asian Americans are fairly well educated and **affluent**. Three out of four Asian youths graduate from high school, compared to less than one out of two for African Americans and Latinos. Asian Americans also have the highest percentage of college graduates, and they earn more doctoral degrees than any other minority group. Many Asian Americans have entered professional fields. As a result, the average income in 1998 for Asian American families was over $4,000 higher than the national average.

—Adapted from Divine, Breen, Fredrickson, & Williams, *The American Story*, pp. 1085–86.

_____9. The best statement of the implied central idea for the passage is _____
   a. Overall, Asian immigrants are thriving in America.
   b. Asian Americans are intelligent and hardworking.
   c. Asian Americans are the fastest-growing group of people coming into the United States.
   d. Asian families encourage their children.

_____10. What logical inference can you make from the information in this paragraph?
   a. Asian Americans are smarter than other Americans.
   b. Asian immigrants face fewer problems adjusting to life in America than other minority groups.
   c. Asian Americans value education.
   d. Asian Americans have a stronger work ethic than any other group.

Name_____Section_____Date_____Score (number correct) _____ x 10 = _____

Directions: Read the passage below. Decide if the following statements are valid inferences that are firmly based on the information in the passage.

[1]On an everyday basis, all of us deal with a set of issues and events ranging from personal issues (such as job or school stress, financial needs, and family demands) to global issues (such as world hunger and world peace).

[2]Often the way we word our ideas reveals our attitudes about our own sense of power. [3]According to Stephen R. Covey, author of *The Seven Habits of Highly Effective People*, most of us have either a "proactive" or "reactive" attitude. [4]For example, a reactive student who is constantly late with assignments might say, "I wish I could be on time with my assignments, but I just can't help it; something always comes up." [5]In contrast, a proactive student thinks, "I am going to set up a schedule so that I can get my assignments completed on time."

[6]A proactive individual understands that he or she must take responsibility for his or her own actions. [7]For proactive people, circumstances do not dictate success—they themselves do. [8]Feelings do not rule behaviors, and decisions are based on values and goals. [9]A perfect example of the difference between reactive and proactive attitudes can be seen in the different ways people think of love. [10]A reactive person thinks of love primarily as a feeling. [11]Thus as the feelings of love diminish, the commitment to the relationship weakens. [12]A proactive person, by contrast, looks at love as an act of will. [13]The decision to be loyal to the commitment stays strong even if feelings diminish.

_____1.   A reactive person does not take responsibility for his or her actions.
      a.   valid inference
      b.   not a valid inference

_____2.   Proactive people are usually more successful than reactive people.
      a.   valid inference
      b.   not a valid inference

_____3.   Reactive people are more likely to be affected by circumstances (such as the weather) than proactive people are.
      a.   valid inference
      b.   not a valid inference

_____4.   Most people are proactive.
      a.   valid inference
      b.   not a valid inference

_____5.   "I can" is a proactive statement.
      a.   valid inference
      b.   not a valid inference

157

____6. Proactive people are not affected by what others think of them.
     a. valid inference
     b. not a valid inference

____7. Events do not hurt us, but how we respond to them can.
     a. valid inference
     b. not a valid inference

____8. Once a reactive person, always a reactive person.
     a. valid inference
     b. not a valid inference

____9. "I choose" is a reactive statement.
     a. valid inference
     b. not a valid inference

Directions: Read the following paragraphs from college textbooks, and determine the most logical inference for each selection.

When we watch the ways individual families interact with their infants or young children and then follow the children over time to see which ones later have high or low IQs, we can begin to get some sense of the kinds of specific family interactions that foster higher scores. At least five dimensions of family interaction or stimulation seem to make a difference. Families with higher-IQ children tend to do the following:

1. They provide an *interesting and complex physical environment* for the child, including play materials that are appropriate for the child's age and developmental level.
2. They are *emotionally responsive* to and *involved* with their child. They respond warmly and contingently to the child's behavior, smiling when the child smiles, answering the child's questions, and in myriad ways reacting to the child's cues.
3. They *talk to their child* often, using language that is descriptively rich and accurate. And when they interact with the child, they operate in what Vygotsky referred to as the *zone of proximal development,* aiming their conversation, their questions, and their assistance at a level that is just above the level the child could manage on her own, thus helping the child to master new skills.
4. They avoid *excessive restrictiveness*, punitiveness, or control, instead giving the child room to explore, even opportunities to make mistakes.
5. They *expect* their child to do well and to develop rapidly. They emphasize and press for school achievement.

—Bee, *Lifespan Development,* 2nd ed., pp. 182–183.

____10. Which statement is a valid inference based upon the details in the passage?
     a. Effective parents rely on experts to teach their children.
     b. Effective parents would probably punish a child for a poor report card.
     c. Effective parents enrich a child's vocabulary by using descriptive and accurate language when they talk to the child.
     d. Effective parents expect their children to be seen and not heard.

Name_____Section_____Date_____Score (number correct)_____ x 10 = _____

A. Directions: Read the passage below. Decide if the following statements are valid inferences that are firmly based on the information in the passage.

With a dark scowl on his face, Jerome marched down the driveway to his car. Violently jerking on the handle, he flung open the driver's door, got in, and slammed the door shut. He gunned the engine to life and squealed out of the driveway in reverse. He ground the gears as he shifted into drive; then he peeled off, leaving a burn of rubber on the road as he roared away.

_____1. Jerome is angry.
   a.   valid inference
   b.   not a valid inference

_____2. Jerome is a skilled driver.
   a.   valid inference
   b.   not a valid inference

_____3. Jerome is allowing his emotions to affect his driving.
   a.   valid inference
   b.   not a valid inference

_____4. Jerome often becomes angry.
   a.   valid inference
   b.   not a valid inference

B. Directions: Read each of the following groups of sentences, and then select the letter of the accurate inference based on the details presented.

- On the closet door hangs a stunning sea-foam green formal dress with shimmering glass beads and sequins.
- Stephanie sits in front of the mirror, carefully applying her makeup.
- Stephanie's hair is in hot curlers, and she is dressed in her bathrobe and fuzzy blue slippers.

_____5. What can you infer from these details?
   a.   Stephanie is preparing to go to the prom.
   b.   Stephanie is preparing to go to a dance.
   c.   Stephanie is preparing to go out.
   d.   Stephanie is preparing for bed.

- Josh goes to swimming practice every morning from 4:00 to 7:00 a.m.
- Josh goes to history class from 8:00 to 8:50 a.m. three days a week.
- Josh has fallen asleep in history class twice this week.

____6. What can you infer from these details?
- a. History is a difficult course for Josh.
- b. The history teacher is a boring lecturer.
- c. Josh is sick.
- d. Josh needs to get more rest.

- The downhill skier travels at a fast clip along the slope while fans cheer on the sidelines.
- He glides over the finish line.
- When he looks at the clock, the skier sighs heavily, shrugs, and then slumps slightly as he moves to the sidelines.

____7. What can you infer from these details?
- a. The skier has improved his time.
- b. The skier has injured himself on the run.
- c. The skier has won a medal.
- d. The skier is disappointed with his time.

C. Directions: Read the passages below and answer the questions that follow.

A procedure called **angioplasty** (sometimes called balloon angioplasty) is associated with fewer risks and is believed by many experts to be more effective than bypass surgery in selected cardiovascular cases. This procedure is similar to angiography. A needle-thin catheter is threaded through the blocked heart arteries. The catheter has a balloon at the tip, which is inflated to flatten fatty deposits against the artery walls, allowing blood to flow more freely. Angioplasty patients are generally awake but sedated during the procedure and spend only one or two days in the hospital after treatment. Most can return to work within five days. In about 30 percent of all angioplasty patients, the treated arteries become clogged again within six months. Some patients may undergo the procedure as many as three times within a five-year period. Some surgeons argue that given angioplasty's high rate of occurrence, bypass may be a more effective method of treatment.

—Donnatelle, *Health,* 4th ed., pp. 298–299.

____8. Which statement is a valid inference based upon the details in the passage?
- a. Heart bypass surgery is more dangerous than angioplasty.
- b. All surgeons prefer angioplasty.
- c. Angioplasty is the same thing as angiography.
- d. All heart patients have clogged arteries.

Over the years, an emerging pattern of higher risks for cancer among persons who engage (or do not engage) in selected lifestyle variables has captured national attention. In particular, diet, sedentary lifestyle, consumption of alcohol and cigarettes, stress, and other health-related behaviors have provided fertile ground for speculation about risks. Many of the studies supporting these purported risks show associations with lifestyle risks, but they have not been shown conclusively to play a causal role in cancer development.

Likewise, colon and rectal cancer appears to occur more frequently among persons with a high-fat, low-fiber diet; in those who don't eat enough fruits and vegetables; and in those who are inactive; yet we can't say that these behaviors actually will cause cancer. For now, there is compelling evidence that certain actions are clearly associated with a greater than average risk of developing diseases. In any of these situations, apparent increases in risk provide fertile ground for behavior modification.

—Donnatelle, *Health,* 4th ed., p. 300.

_____9. Which statement is a valid inference based upon the details in the passage?
- a. Conclusive evidence reveals a connection between a person's lifestyle and the chances of developing cancer.
- b. A sedentary lifestyle is something many doctors would prescribe.
- c. Many studies fail to support a relationship between lifestyle and cancer.
- d. Behavior modification is recommended for people lacking good dietary and exercise habits who might be at risk of developing cancer.

In 1610 Galileo had been given the post of lecturer in philosophy at the University of Florence, because up to then his discoveries had not been in direct conflict with church teachings. But with his new findings, he published a letter in which he announced Copernicus had been right all along. Pope Paul V was angered by this public admission and advised Galileo to renounce his belief that the sun, not the earth, was the center of the universe. The scientist promised to do so, but in 1630 he again defended the Copernican theory in a book, which was immediately banned, and was summoned to appear before the religious authorities. Threatened with excommunication and death, he declared publicly that the earth did not move around the sun and spent the rest of his days as a prisoner, forbidden to write. (A traditional legend is that even as he was denying his former position, he crossed his fingers behind his back and whispered, "Yet it *does* move!")

—Janaro & Altshuler, *The Art of Being Human,* 6th ed., p. 52.

_____10. Which statement is a valid inference based upon the details in the passage?
- a. Galileo renounced his belief about the solar system because he was afraid.
- b. Galileo's belief about the sun was counter to what Copernicus believed.
- c. Galileo was relieved when he was forbidden to write.
- d. Galileo remained supportive of church teachings, even in private.

Name_____ Section _____ Date _____ Score (number correct) _____ x 10 = _____

A. Directions: Read the passage below. Decide if the following statements are valid inferences that are firmly based on the information in the passage.

William Byrd II (1674–1744) was a successful Tidewater planter. He felt at home in both London and Virginia, the state in which he was born. In 1728, at the height of his political power, Byrd agreed to help survey a boundary in dispute between North Carolina and Virginia. During his long trip through the backcountry, Byrd kept a detailed journal. His lively record of daily events is now thought of as a classic piece of early American literature. He met many highly independent people. For example, as soon as he left the world of tobacco plantations behind, he met a self-styled **"hermit"** living in the woods. The hermit, an Englishman, seemed to prefer the freedoms of the wild to the limits set by society.

—Divine, Breen, Fredrickson, & Williams, *The American Story*, p. 105.

_____1. William Byrd lived in eighteenth-century America.
     a. valid inference
     b. not a valid inference

_____2. William Byrd's journal was a record of what he saw while on his journey.
     a. valid inference
     b. not a valid inference

_____3. One of the main crops in North Carolina and Virginia was tobacco.
     a. valid inference
     b. not a valid inference

_____4. The tobacco plantations were found in the back country.
     a. valid inference
     b. not a valid inference

_____5. The hermit was born in America.
     a. valid inference
     b. not a valid inference

B. Directions: Read each of the following groups of sentences, and then select the letter of the accurate inference based on the details presented.

- The 20 airmen move with resolve toward their jets in the predawn hours.
- Although the jets' noses have been painted with a picture representing each pilot, the actual names of the flyers have been removed for this mission.
- On one side of the runway, tearful family members and friends are clustered, waving American flags.

_____6. The most logical inference based upon the details in the sentences is
    a. The pilots are arriving after an absence of many months.
    b. The pilots are on a routine practice mission.
    c. The pilots are leaving for a difficult mission.
    d. The pilots are nervous about their assignment.

- People are crowded into the card section of the grocery store.
- Heart-shaped balloons are in abundance near the checkout stand.
- Red-foiled pots of tulips line shelves in the florist section of the store.

_____7. The most logical inference based upon the details in the sentences is
    a. Christmas is approaching.
    b. Valentine's Day is near.
    c. People are looking for ways to cheer their depressed friends.
    d. The grocery store caters to wealthy patrons.

- In the bookstore coffee shop, Melissa orders herbal tea with soy milk.
- She sits down to study her selections for purchase: *OM Yoga* and *Nutrition and Edible Flowers*.
- She sports well-worn jogging shoes, sweat pants, and a T-shirt that says, "Pain is weakness leaving the body."

_____8. The most logical inference based upon the details in the sentences is
    a. Melissa is an avid jogger.
    b. Melissa has been practicing yoga for many years.
    c. Melissa is thinking of taking up a new exercise program.
    d. Melissa has an interest in nutrition and exercise.

C. Directions: Read the passages below and answer the questions that follow.

The founder of classical criminology is the seventeenth-century Italian nobleman and professor of law Cesare Beccaria (1738–1794). Beccaaria published the first book to advocate fundamentally reforming Europe's judicial and penal systems. The book, titled *Dei Delitti e della Pene* (On Crimes and Punishment), was an impassioned plea to make the criminal justice system rational in the sense that it was based on humanistic principles and an appeal to reason.

Beccaria's philosophy contrasted with many common practices in seventeenth-century Europe. For example, during the 1700s, the penalties imposed by judges were quite harsh, and punishment was a source of public entertainment. Torture was often used to extract confessions from suspects.

—Ellis & Walsh, *Criminology,* p. 83.

163

_____9. Which statement is a valid inference based upon the details in the passage?
   a. Cesare Beccaria was a ruthless, vengeful ruler.
   b. Cesare Beccaria sought to change the justice system because it was unfair.
   c. Cesare Beccaria sought laws that instilled justice rather than revenge. Although torture was used in other European countries, it was never used in Italy.
   d. Torture was used as a punishment only in Italy.

Russian psychologist Lev Vygotsky, who was born the same year as Piaget [1896] but died at the early age of 38, is normally thought of as belonging to the cognitive-development camp, but he placed emphasis somewhat differently. In particular, he was convinced that complex forms of thinking have their origins in *social* interactions rather than in the child's private explorations. According to Vygotsky, children's learning of new cognitive skills is guided by an adult (or a more skilled child, such as an older sibling), who models and structures the child's learning experience, a process called *scaffolding*. Such new learning, Vygotsky suggested, is best achieved in what he called the **zone of proximal development**—that range of tasks that are too hard for the child to do alone but that he can manage with guidance. As the child becomes more skilled, the zone of proximal development steadily shifts upward, including ever-harder tasks.

—Bee, *Lifespan Development,* 2nd ed., p. 37.

_____10. Which statement is a valid inference based upon the details in the passage?
   a. Sometimes parents and teachers try to teach children new skills before they are ready.
   b. Vygotsky believed that children could learn anything if they are left to explore on their own.
   c. Vygotsky felt that teachers and parents were unimportant in a child's cognitive development.
   d. Scaffolding teaches children new things by making huge leaps from one stage to another without guidance.

Name_____ Section _____ Date _____ Score (number correct) _____ x 10 = _____

Objective: To identify the claim and support in an argument.

A. Directions: Read all of the statements for each question and choose the claim.

_____1. Which one of the following sentences states the claim for this group of ideas?
   a. People who rent their homes never make money in the transaction, and they are not in control when the monthly payments are increased.
   b. Homeowners can build up equity and eventually show a profit from their investment years later.
   c. People should be encouraged to own a home rather than rent.
   d. People who own their own homes take more pride in their community.

_____2. Which one of the following sentences states the claim for this group of ideas?
   a. Athletes often develop a network that proves advantageous when they begin job hunting.
   b. Participation in sports in college enhances a student's academic and professional life.
   c. Coaches often keep a vigilant eye on their team members' grades, so the athletes often get special academic privileges such as early registration and access to excellent tutors.
   d. Many companies recruit former athletes because of their leadership and team skills.

_____3. Which one of the following sentences states the claim for this group of ideas?
   a. Reading aloud provides an opportunity for parents and young children to sit closely and enjoy some time alone, without the distractions of a TV, video game, or computer.
   b. When parents read aloud to their adolescent children, they are sending the message, "I value you, and I value your education."
   c. Reading aloud to children of all ages builds long-term bonds.
   d. Snuggling with a child during reading time helps to create a sense of security.

B. Directions: Read the paragraph and determine whether the sentences state the claim or support for an argument.

[1]Because they are plentiful and require little land or maintenance, insects are an economical food source. [2]In many countries, eating bugs is a part of the culture's cuisine. [3]Fried grubs, for example, are a tasty treat in Australia. [4]Because they are low in cholesterol, insects make a healthful meal. [5]Many third-world countries also exist on grazing animals. [6]Insects are a viable, healthful food source and should be marketed worldwide.

____4. Sentence 1 states the _____.
     a. claim
     b. support
     c. This sentence is not relevant information.

____5. Sentence 2 states the _____.
     a. claim
     b. support
     c. This sentence is not relevant information.

____6. Sentence 4 states the _____.
     a. claim
     b. support
     c. This sentence is not relevant information.

____7. Sentence 5 states the _____.
     a. claim
     b. support
     c. This sentence is not relevant information.

____8. Sentence 6 states the _____.
     a. claim
     b. support
     c. This sentence is not relevant information.

C. Directions: Read the paragraph and answer the questions that follow.

[1]Injury is not only possible but probable. [2]In the face of this risk, the athlete's heart pounds with excitement, and the thought of turning back is overcome by the anticipation of the thrill ahead. [3]The skateboarder runs his skateboard up the ramp, somersaults in the air, and slams back down at incredible speeds. [4]Many communities frown on skateboarding because of the noise and damage caused to sidewalks and handrails. [5]A young woman stands on the span of a bridge that looms hundreds of feet high. [6]When she jumps, she is counting on her parachute to carry her away from the bridge instead of slamming her into its concrete foundation. [7]She hopes to race toward the ground at speeds over 60 miles an hour, and she plans to pull the cord in just enough time to swoop gently to the ground. [8]She is BASE jumping. [9]Participation in extreme sports like snowboarding, sky diving, ice climbing, skateboarding, and BASE jumping is on the rise.

____9. Which of the following claims is adequately supported by the evidence?
     a. Extreme sports appeal only to crazy people.
     b. Extreme sports should not be covered by insurance.
     c. Extreme sports attract athletes who want to experience danger and excitement.
     d. Extreme sports should be banned.

____10. Which sentence is not relevant to the claim?
     a. sentence 1
     b. sentence 3
     c. sentence 4
     d. sentence 9

166

Name_____ Section _____ Date _____ Score (number correct) _____ x 10 = _____

Objective: To identify the claim and support in an argument.

A. Directions: Read all of the statements for each question and choose the claim.

_____1. Which one of the following sentences states the claim for this group of ideas?
    a. To graduate from high school in the 1940s, my grandfather was required to take a civics course, which included how to plan a budget, balance a checkbook, and adhere to a savings plan.
    b. Schools in the 1940s also insisted that students understand the importance of voting and the way to get laws passed or changed to improve the quality of life in a community.
    c. Local school boards should require that all high school students successfully complete a course in civics.
    d. Many students today don't know how to plan a budget or balance a checkbook.

_____2. Which one of the following sentences states the claim for this group of ideas?
    a. Most employers select and hire their employees by networking.
    b. Hiring the right person requires more than a good ad in the newspaper or on the Internet.
    c. One of the things many professionals are coached in is joining the right group, such as a local Rotary Club, which provides a broader network for locating future candidates.
    d. Many career centers counsel their clients to form as many networks as possible.

_____3. Which one of the following sentences states the claim for this group of ideas?
    a. Give the candidate a skills test to ensure that he or she can do what is indicated on the application.
    b. During the interview, allow other employees who will be affected by the new hire to ask questions.
    c. An experienced employer should provide opportunities for the applicant to demonstrate his or her skills to more than just one supervisor.
    d. Include a team of supervisors and fellow workers on the hiring committee.

B. Directions: Read the following outline of a point and its supports. Decide if each support is relevant to the claim or if it is not relevant to the claim.

Claim: Human use of fossil fuels is the main cause of acid rain.

Support:

_____4. The acid in acid rain comes from two kinds of air pollutants that are created by burning fossil fuels—sulfur dioxide (SO_2) and nitrogen oxides (NO_x).
    a. relevant
    b. not relevant

Support:

_____5. Acid rain toxins come mainly from industrial smokestacks and automobile, truck, and bus exhaust pipes—all of which rely on fossil fuels for power.
    a.   relevant
    b.   not relevant

Support:

_____6. Although not a fossil fuel, wood, when burned, also emits pollutants that cause acid rain.
    a.   relevant
    b.   not relevant

Support:

_____7. The harmful effects of acid rain have been reported worldwide.
    a.   relevant
    b.   not relevant

Support:

_____8. Acid rain damages both wildlife and structures built by humans.
    a.   relevant
    b.   not relevant

Support:

_____9. Driving cars that are battery-powered would eliminate some of the pollutants that cause acid rain.
    a.   relevant
    b.   not relevant

Support:

_____10. Nuclear power could replace the use of fossil fuels and cut down on acid rain.
    a.   relevant
    b.   not relevant

CHAPTER 12: THE BASICS OF ARGUMENT
Lab 12.3 REVIEW TEST 1

Name_____ Section _____ Date _____ Score (number correct) _____ x 10 = _____

A. Directions: Read all of the statements for each question and choose the claim.

_____1. Which one of the following sentences states the claim for this group of ideas?
    a. Basketball players must be able to sprint up and down the court for two and a half hours.
    b. Basketball has the longest playing season of all the major sports.
    c. Basketball players are some of the best all-round athletes.
    d. Unlike any other athletes, basketball players must use speed, endurance, and accuracy skills at the same time.

_____2. Which one of the following sentences states the claim for this group of ideas?
    a. Many video games encourage violence.
    b. Many violent video games put the player in the role of seeking and killing victims.
    c. Some experts believe that role-playing is an important step in becoming violent.
    d. Other experts fear that the violence in the games makes players think of violence as fun.

_____3. Which one of the following sentences states the claim for this group of ideas?
    a. Marijuana has proven medical benefits for cancer patients.
    b. Marijuana stimulates the appetite and eases the discomfort of those who suffer with nausea from chemotherapy.
    c. Marijuana should be legalized.
    d. The current ban on marijuana has not stopped its sale and use.

B. Directions: Read the following outline of a point and its supports. Decide if each support is relevant to the claim or if it is not relevant to the claim.

Claim: You can improve your study time at home.

Support

_____4. Sit toward the front of the classroom.
    a. relevant
    b. not relevant

_____5. Have supplies nearby, such as paper, pens, pencils, class notes, and textbooks.
    a. relevant
    b. not relevant

_____6. Get rid of external distractions by shutting off the radio and television or moving to a quiet location.
    a. relevant
    b. not relevant

C. Directions: Read the following outline of a point and its supports. Decide if each support is relevant to the claim or if it is not relevant to the claim.

Claim: Meditation is an excellent way to relax and manage stress.

Support

_____7. Meditation uses deep breathing to release tension and relax muscles.
      a.   relevant
      b.   not relevant

Support

_____8. Anyone can practice meditation because it easy to learn and has no cost.
      a.   relevant
      b.   not relevant

Support

_____9. Meditation also turns the mind away from problems and focuses on inner peace.
      a.   relevant
      b.   not relevant

Support

_____10. Many people resist using meditation as a stress-management tool because they think it is a religious practice.
      a.   relevant
      b.   not relevant

170

Name_____ Section _____ Date _____ Score (number correct) _____ x 10 = _____

Ritalin: Use or Abuse?

Doctors prescribe it, parents pass it out to children, and school nurses supervise the administration of it because all believe the pill will calm children and stop their disruptive behavior. It is methylphenidate. Best known by the brand name Ritalin, methylphenidate was introduced in 1956 and is a stimulant in the same class as amphetamines. Experts agree that it affects the midbrain, the part of the brain that controls impulses.

Advocates of Ritalin assert that the drug is a blessing and that it has helped those with attention deficit/hyperactivity disorder (ADHD) to concentrate. People diagnosed with ADHD are unable to sit still, plan ahead, finish tasks, or be fully aware of what's going on around them. To their family, classmates, or coworkers, they seem to exist in a cyclone of disorganized or harried activity. One of the most common mental disorders among children, it affects 3% to 5% of all children, perhaps as many as 2 million children in the United States. Two to three times more boys than girls are affected, and on average, at least one child in every classroom in the United States needs help for the disorder.

Ritalin allows the patient to focus better on the task at hand. Besides its use in treating the symptoms of ADHD, Ritalin is also prescribed for mild to moderate depression and in some cases of emotional withdrawal among elderly people. Initially Ritalin was used for children who were so restless that they were unreachable and unteachable. The National Institutes of Health support "the efficacy of stimulants and psychosocial treatments for ADHD and the superiority of stimulants relative to psychosocial treatments." The benefits of Ritalin are so strong that advocates say withholding the pills is a form of neglect. Those who claim diet, exercise, or other treatments work just as well are kidding themselves, say believers. A typical parental comment is the following:

> His homework took 3 hours—even with me helping him—to do because his mind was in the sky.
> He was a genius at video games, but not at homework. He was also at the point of being held
> back in school. He shed tears because he could not control himself; he hated the way he acted. I
> was always getting complaints about his spontaneous outbursts. And then he took Ritalin—and
> everything changed.

But the situation is not all rosy. Critics say doctors who work with teachers to keep boisterous children in line misdiagnose students. As awareness of ADHD has grown, the characterization of the disorder now encompasses a much broader range of behaviors—an increasing number of children seem to have conditions that meet the definition of ADHD.

Ritalin production has increased by more than 700% since 1990. Since then disorders for which Ritalin is prescribed have jumped an average of 21% per year. Over the past five years alone, the number of prescriptions for Ritalin in the United States has jumped to 11.4 million from 4.5 million, including about 11% of all boys in the United States. Researchers claim a disturbing reliance upon the drug to solve problems that have other solutions.

Ritalin is classified as a Schedule II drug—on a par with cocaine, morphine, and metamphetamines—thus there is potential for abuse or dependence. Ritalin is widely misused by drug addicts, and it has associated with it a large number of suicides and emergency room admissions. The National Institutes of Health caution that "stimulant treatments may not 'normalize' the entire range of behavior problems, and children under treatment may still manifest a higher level of some behavior problems than normal children." They also note that there are no long-term studies testing stimulants or psychosocial treatments lasting several years.

Of course, an ADHD diagnosis can and often does lead to medication, special education facilities, and parental support groups. Today, children and teenagers with ADHD may be placed in a special classroom and eventually get non-timed college admission tests—about 40,000 SAT tests are administered this way each year. Are the ADHD diagnosis and the Ritalin treatment being used for the wrong reasons? By overzealous parents? By well-meaning physicians?

Is Ritalin effective? Yes, it is. Can it help children and teenagers with ADHD? Yes, it can. Are mistakes made in diagnosing ADHD? Of course. Is there overdiagnosis? Yes. Overdiagnosis usually occurs when a doctor is inexperienced, untrained, pressured, or predisposed to "find" ADHD. We need careful controlled research into the impact and long-term effects of Ritalin—and those studies are still a few years away. We also need physician, teacher, and parent education into ADHD and the use of Ritalin.

—Lofton & Brannon, *Psychology*, 8th ed., pp. 100–101.

_____1. The topic of the passage is _____.
- a. reasons Ritalin should continue to be prescribed by physicians
- b. reasons Ritalin should not continue to be prescribed by physicians
- c. the advantages and disadvantages of Ritalin
- d. the increase in hyperactivity in the U.S. population

_____2. The purpose of the passage is to _____.
- a. persuade parents to seek professional help for their hyperactive children
- b. inform people of the positive and negative aspects of Ritalin
- c. persuade physicians to exercise caution when prescribing Ritalin
- d. inform adults about the misuses of Ritalin

_____3. The claim of the argument advanced in the passage is that _____.
- a. conflicting information about the benefits and problems of Ritalin use indicate that more study and caution are required
- b. critics of the use of Ritalin should rethink their position, since there are so many advantages to using the drug
- c. proponents of Ritalin use have failed to consider the disadvantages of the drug
- d. people should learn self-discipline and alternate methods of handling hyperactivity, rather than relying on Ritalin, which is viewed as a dangerous "quick fix"

_____4. The audience to which this selection is aimed would include all of the following *except* _____.
- a. pediatricians
- b. educators
- c. parents
- d. entertainers

_____5. "Ritalin allows the patient to focus better on the task at hand."
      a.   This statement is relevant to the claim.
      b.   This statement is not relevant to the claim.

_____6. "Besides its use in treating the symptoms of ADHD, Ritalin is also prescribed for mild to moderate depression and in some cases of emotional withdrawal among elderly people."
      a.   This statement is relevant to the claim.
      b.   This statement is not relevant to the claim.

_____7. "Initially Ritalin was used for children who were so restless that they were unreachable and unteachable."
      a.   This statement is relevant to the claim.
      b.   This statement is not relevant to the claim.

_____8. "The National Institutes of Health support 'the efficacy of stimulants and psychosocial treatments for ADHD and the superiority of stimulants relative to psychosocial treatments.'"
      a.   This statement is relevant to the claim.
      b.   This statement is not relevant to the claim.

_____9. "The benefits of Ritalin are so strong that advocates say withholding the pills is a form of neglect."
      a.   This statement is relevant to the claim.
      b.   This statement is not relevant to the claim.

_____10. "Those who claim diet, exercise, or other treatments work just as well are kidding themselves, say believers."
      a.   This statement is relevant to the claim.
      b.   This statement is not relevant to the claim.

Name _____ Section _____ Date _____ Score (number correct) _____ x 10 = _____

A. Directions: Read all of the statements for each question and choose the claim.

_____1. Which one of the following sentences states the claim for this group of ideas?
    a. NBA basketball star Michael Jordan earned around $38 million in 2002.
    b. Golf champion Tiger Woods earned around $69 million in 2002.
    c. Michael Jordan and Tiger Woods are both minorities.
    d. Minority male athletes earn some of the highest salaries in America.

_____2. Which one of the following sentences states the claim for this group of ideas?
    a. David Small constantly sent letters that were full of mistakes to clients.
    b. David Small's work files were unorganized and incomplete.
    c. David Small was given several opportunities to improve his work.
    d. David Small was fired for good reasons.

_____3. Which one of the following sentences states the claim for this group of ideas?
    a. Many characters in the movie drink alcohol; they drink beer, vodka, champagne, wine, and mixed drinks.
    b. The movie is based on the idea that couples sleep around constantly and without guilt.
    c. The movie *How to Lose a Guy in Ten Days* does not offer good role models for young people.
    d. Crude language and curse words are used nearly 50 times.

_____4. Which one of the following sentences states the claim for this group of ideas adapted from the college text, DeVito, *Messages,* 4th ed., p. 183?
    a. Many people simply don't know how to express anger without using violence, blame, or accusations.
    b. Some people feel that men have more of a problem expressing their emotions than do women.
    c. Perhaps the most important obstacle to effectively communicating emotions is the lack of interpersonal skills
    d. Others cannot express love; they literally cannot say, "I love you."

B. Directions: Read the following outline of a point and its supports. Decide if each support is relevant to the claim or if it is not relevant to the claim.

Claim: Education is critical in the early prevention and treatment of diabetes.

Support

____5. To live with diabetes, a person must learn a large amount of information about the body, the disease, and its treatments.
   a. relevant
   b. not relevant

Support

____6. Decisions must be made every day about meal-planning, exercise, and drugs.
   a. relevant
   b. not relevant

Support

____7. Funding is needed to find a cure for diabetes.
   a. relevant
   b. not relevant

Support

____8. Lifestyle changes can delay the onset of diabetes.
   a. relevant
   b. not relevant

Support

____9. Weight loss, a healthy diet, and regular exercise reduce the chance of developing diabetes by half.
   a. relevant
   b. not relevant

Support

____10. Many famous people suffer with diabetes.
   a. relevant
   b. not relevant

CHAPTER 12: THE BASICS OF ARGUMENT
Lab 12.6 MASTERY TEST 2

Name_____ Section _____ Date _____ Score (number correct) _____ x 10 = _____

A. Directions: Read all of the statements for each question and choose the claim.

_____1. Which one of the following sentences states the claim for this group of ideas?
 a. A recent study by the Partnership for a Drug-Free America showed that 45 percent of youths aged 12 to 18 saw a great risk in using the drug Ecstasy.
 b. In 2001, over 5,000 emergency-room visits were related to Ecstasy use.
 c. In 2002, 253 emergency-room visits were related to Ecstasy use.
 d. Although many teenagers see the risk of using Ecstasy, the dangers the drug poses to youth should not be ignored.

_____2. Which one of the following sentences states the claim for this group of ideas?
 a. Never rely solely on eyewitness accounts, which can be biased or faulty.
 b. You should use these guidelines to help you decide when an employee should be fired for theft.
 c. Meet with the accused to get all the facts; there may be a reasonable explanation.
 d. Weigh the employee's offense against other disciplinary problems to avoid a harsh overreaction.

_____3. Which one of the following sentences states the claim for this group of ideas?
 a. Cloning is an imperfect scientific process that can result in problems in the cloned animals.
 b. Most attempts at cloning end in failure because the fetuses have oversized organs in the womb or are born stillborn.
 c. Other cloned animals have been born twice as large as normal.
 d. A veterinary exam confirmed that a 6-year-old cloned sheep had a progressive lung disease.

_____4. Which one of the following sentences states the claim for this group of ideas adapted from the college text, DeVito, *Messages: Building Interpersonal Communication Skills,* 4th ed., p. 331?
 a. Sexual harassment in school has harmful effects on students who are victims.
 b. Students who have been victims of sexual harassment in school have trouble paying attention, have trouble studying, and earn low grades.
 c. Many of these students have difficulty speaking out in class, don't want to go to school, or think about changing schools.
 d. Victims of sexual harassment are often too afraid to speak to policemen.

B. Directions: Read the paragraphs and answer the questions that follow.

[1]Have you noticed that mounting malpractice insurance costs have pressured doctors to limit their time with patients by requiring an allotted number of face-to-face office visits a day? [2]Insurance companies have acquired an inordinate amount of power that affects everyone, a situation that now calls for a dramatic change. [3]The high cost of malpractice insurance has actually prompted some doctors to leave medicine and find jobs in other fields. [4]Some doctors have turned to law, while others have left the professional ranks altogether. [5]Also, as a result of rising insurance costs and a reduction in the services some companies cover, many patients postpone or cancel needed exams or procedures.

_____5. Which sentence states the claim of the argument?
    a. sentence 1
    b. sentence 2
    c. sentence 3
    d. sentence 4

_____6. Which sentence is *not* a valid support for the claim?
    a. sentence 2
    b. sentence 3
    c. sentence 4
    d. sentence 5

[1]Creating a new reservoir in the eastern part of the state will reduce the shad population, which is an important contributor to the state's economic growth. [2]As it now stands, the proposal for a new reservoir would have a negative impact on the entire state. [3]It would displace many people from their homes. [4]It would also destroy important Indian ancestral land, including the burial grounds for the Mattaponi Indians. [5]Real estate prices would rise in the area, contributing dollars to the needed tax base.

_____7. Which sentence states the claim of the argument?
    a. sentence 1
    b. sentence 2
    c. sentence 3
    d. sentence 4

_____8. Which sentence is *not* a valid support for the claim?
    a. sentence 2
    b. sentence 3
    c. sentence 4
    d. sentence 5

[1]The traffic signal at the junction of Main Trail and Granada Boulevard makes the intersection dangerous. [2]Whoever programmed the light is stupid. [3]Granada Boulevard is a heavily traveled four-lane state road. [4]Main Trail is the entrance to a large residential neighborhood. [5]To enter the neighborhood, traffic must turn left. [6]The traffic signal is programmed to turn green and allow the left turn into the neighborhood. [7]However, after only two or three cars turn, the left turn signal turns red. [8]Cars are forced to wait at the red light long after there is no more oncoming traffic. [9]To avoid sitting through a five-minute red light, many drivers rush through the signal as it turns yellow or run the light after it has turned red. [10]The timing of the light encourages reckless driving.

_____9. Which sentence states the claim of the argument?
    a. sentence 1
    b. sentence 2
    c. sentence 3
    d. sentence 4

_____10. Which sentence is NOT a valid support for the claim?
    a. sentence 2
    b. sentence 4
    c. sentence 7
    d. sentence 9

178

Name_____ Section _____ Date _____ Score (number correct) _____ x 10 = _____

Objective: To identify fallacies of logic and propaganda techniques.

A. Directions: Choose the fallacy used in each of the following items.

_____1. I like R & B music, because it's my favorite.
      a. begging the question
      b. personal attack
      c. straw man
      d. either-or

_____2. My record is the record and it represents my excellence in the field because it is so good.
      a. begging the question
      b. personal attack
      c. straw man
      d. either-or

_____3. Why would anyone vote for that candidate? He is an overzealous tree-hugger who hasn't a clue about how to run a government.
      a. begging the question
      b. personal attack
      c. straw man
      d. either-or

_____4. Paul is a generous and courageous man because he is a fire fighter, and all fire fighters are brave.
      a. begging the question
      b. personal attack
      c. straw man
      d. either-or

_____5. Governor Rock Slide is an excellent politician because he is also a movie star.
      a. begging the question
      b. personal attack
      c. straw man
      d. either-or

B. Directions: Identify the propaganda technique used in each of the following items.

_____ 6. Are you tired of being told what to do? Do you want a venue that is safe for expressing your own views? Come join the Young Democrats and hook up with open-minded, progressive-thinking members.
    a. plain folk
    b. bandwagon
    c. testimonial
    d. name-calling

_____ 7. "Ever since I started eating Maine blueberries, I've had more energy and more clarity of thought. There is nothing better than the natural properties of this home-grown product, and I promise you will enjoy similar benefits as well."
    a. plain folk
    b. bandwagon
    c. testimonial
    d. name-calling

_____ 8. The advertisement displays two sandwiches. One is a large, juicy double cheeseburger. The other is a small, flat burger on a bun. The caption reads, "Theirs? Ours? You decide."
    a. plain folk
    b. bandwagon
    c. testimonial
    d. name-calling

_____ 9. Mr. Santiago works diligently in his yard each weekend to touch up the paint on the house, clean the gutters, rake the yard, plant flowers, and wash windows. Recently he said, "I have pride in my home, and I work hard to make sure it looks good so that it is a reflection of the order in my personal life."
    a. transfer
    b. glittering generalities
    c. card stacking
    d. testimonial

_____ 10. A representative of a computer software firm offers a presentation on his company's product and explains that using the program for a college's student information system will facilitate record-keeping and provide opportunities for online registration. He also mentions that the program has been used successfully in many businesses across the country. However, he fails to tell the group that the company is currently in litigation with the community college system in another state because it did not dovetail easily to the academic arena and had previously only been an effective human resource program for some national businesses.
    a. transfer
    b. glittering generalities
    c. card stacking
    d. bandwagon

Name_____ Section _____ Date _____ Score (number correct) _____ x 10 = _____

Objective: To identify fallacies of logic and propaganda techniques.

A. Directions: Choose the fallacy used in each of the following items.

____1. My philosophy professor is so incompetent and so boring, but what can you expect from a man
with gray hair?
a. begging the question
b. personal attack
c. straw man
d. either-or

____2. Channel 51 is the best TV station because it offers the most enjoyable entertainment for everyone.
a. begging the question
b. personal attack
c. straw man
d. false cause

____3. Although my opponent is a very distinguished citizen, he cannot possibly understand the needs of
real Americans. He owns seven estates around the world, one that was imported from Italy stone
by stone. He obviously has no clue about the real world.
a. begging the question
b. personal attack
c. straw man
d. false comparison

____4. Either vote for a more efficient public transportation system, or endure the high costs of gasoline.
a. either-or
b. begging the question
b. personal attack
c. straw man

____5. The Internet is just like a lawless society in that there is little or no regulation. The Internet is just
as dangerous as a society without laws.
a. begging the question
b. personal attack
c. straw man
d. false comparison

B. Directions: Identify the propaganda technique used in each of the following items.

_____6. Everyone in Hampton is behind Jane Simon for Mayor. Shouldn't you be part of this winning team?
   a. name-calling
   b. testimonial
   c. band wagon
   d. transfer

_____7. Mr. Hyle is a well-respected professor of environmental science at the local college. Since Mr. Hyle is well-known and respected both locally and around the state, he will likely gain many votes for his endorsement of Spencer Turner for city manager.
   a. glittering generalities
   b. testimonial
   c. card stacking
   d. band wagon

_____8. After a rousing speech to the new cadets, General Shook rolled up his sleeves, donned an apron and handed out hot dogs and hamburgers to the parents of the new recruits.
   a. plain folks
   b. name-calling
   c. glittering generalities
   d. transfer

_____9. The environmentalist group SAVE THE SPECIES, in its attempt to prevent a planned development from destroying the natural habitat of a rare tree frog, produces a television ad with an official looking "scientist" standing in the middle of a biology lab explaining the dramatic consequences of altering the food chain by destroying this habitat.
   a. testimonial
   b. glittering generalities
   c. plain folks
   d. transfer

_____10. An ad by local protestors who are angry about the new "No Smoking" ban in restaurants states in large, bold letters: Don't let them take your rights away!
   a. name-calling
   b. plain folks
   c. glittering generalities
   d. testimonial

182

Name_____ Section _____ Date _____ Score (number correct) _____ x 10 = _____

A. Directions: Identify the fallacy used in each of the following items.

_____1. Although the drainage ditches in our residential areas are unsightly and unhealthy, local officials refuse to authorize city workers to lay drainage pipes to fill them in because they don't care about issues that affect the environment.
    a. begging the question
    b. personal attack
    c. straw man
    d. false comparison

_____2. The play was replete with profanity, and it is obvious that the theater department intends to undermine the family values in our community.
    a. begging the question
    b. personal attack
    c. straw man
    d. either-or

_____3. Consumers who buy fur and leather products are nothing but a bunch of hypocrites who have no respect for nature.
    a. begging the question
    b. personal attack
    c. straw man
    d. false comparison

_____4. Currently there is a six-year waiting list for anyone with a mental disability to move into a group home. Why are our state politicians more concerned about providing tax cuts for the rich than helping those in need?
    a. false cause
    b. personal attack
    c. either-or
    d. straw man

_____5. President Smith eliminated four major programs at our college so he could fund the building of new dormitories and landscape the grounds with fountains and flowers. He is clearly looking out for himself and does not care about this institution; he wants only to pad his résumé, so he can run a successful campaign for governor.
    a. personal attack
    b. begging the question
    c. either-or
    d. false comparison

183

B. Directions: Identify the propaganda technique used in each of the following items.

_____6. The automobile advertisement displaying a woman in work clothes states: "This is Eleanor. She is a mother and a grandmother. She is also one of our assembly-line technicians, and her job is to make sure our cars are safe for her parents, for her children, and for YOU."
- a. plain folks
- b. bandwagon
- c. testimonial
- d. name-calling

_____7. The advertisement displays a photograph of Olympic swimmers from four countries as they wait on deck, listening to music using the same earphones and CD player. The caption reads: "Join the winners. Own one, too!"
- a. plain folks
- b. glittering generalities
- c. testimonial
- d. name-calling

_____8. "He lied in college. He lied in law school. He lied in the Pentagon in 1990. And he lied to you last year. Ah, that must be what the "L" stands for in John L. Farber. A vote for me is a vote for honesty."
- a. plain folks.
- b. bandwagon.
- c. testimonial
- d. name-calling

_____9. A young man appears at your door with a clipboard in hand and says, "All of your neighbors have signed this petition to endorse speed bumps on the neighborhood streets. You don't want to be left out, do you?"
- a. plain folks.
- b. bandwagon.
- c. testimonial
- d. name-calling

C. Directions: Read the following fictitious advertisement. Identify the detail that was **omitted** from the advertisement for the purpose of card-stacking.

_____10. Blue Oasis is the most refreshing bottled water on the market. Not only does it quench your thirst, but it will also compensate for any mineral deficiencies your body may have. Enjoy the guarantee that you are drinking our safe, clean, and untainted water that is cleansed by nature's own best purifier— from the underground springs and rocks through which it flows. For generations, our water has been particularly linked to health and well-being.
- a. Drinking water helps to keep the body hydrated.
- b. Bottled water is less regulated than tap water. There are few if any restrictions on it.
- c. Water is a far better choice for children than drinks sweetened with sugar.
- d. Water plays an essential role in good hydration before and after heavy exercise.

184

Name_____Section_____Date_____Score (number correct)_____ x 10 =_____

A. Directions: Identify the fallacy used in each of the following items.

____1. Our senator is a proponent of building a stronger navy and increasing the number of nuclear submarines, which means that he is more interested in serving his constituents than ensuring that we focus on world peace.
    a. begging the question
    b. personal attack
    c. straw man
    d. either-or

____2. The mayor is a known womanizer, so how can we trust him to provide leadership in our city?
    a. begging the question
    b. personal attack
    c. straw man
    d. either-or

____3. Athletes should be given special treatment on campus because they are students worthy of extra benefits.
    a. begging the question
    b. personal attack
    c. straw man
    d. either-or

____4. How can you say you have grown up? Look at the way you spend your money, always buying expensive toys and impractical vehicles!
    a. begging the question
    b. personal attack
    c. straw man
    d. either-or

____5. Circumventing the law is not unethical if it is legal.
    a. begging the question
    b. personal attack
    c. straw man
    d. either-or

B. Directions: Identify the propaganda technique used in each of the following items.

_____ 6. When orchestrating his candidate's photo shoot, a campaign manager staged the family in front of a tree in the front yard, rather than on the back deck that overlooked the river. He then had his candidate remove his gold cuff links and Rolex watch, roll up his sleeves, and shoot some baskets with his sons. He was using which strategy to promote his candidate?
   a. plain folk
   b. bandwagon
   c. testimonial
   d. name-calling

_____ 7. Before the interview with the presidential candidate, the camera captures him running barefoot on a public beach with his dog and children nearby. He wears rolled up khaki pants, a wrinkled blue work shirt, and an Atlanta Braves ball cap. This photo shoot uses which strategy?
   a. plain folk
   b. bandwagon
   c. testimonial
   d. name-calling

_____ 8. A local TV station calls a water theme park supervisor to apprise the management that they secretly took a water sample of their pool and discovered the chlorine levels there are dangerously low and they are planning to air an expose of the business. What they will not mention in their report, however, is that chlorine burns off in sunlight, and their sample was exposed for three hours outside before it was tested.
   a. transfer
   b. glittering generalities
   c. card stacking
   d. bandwagon

_____ 9. If he were still here, Ronald Reagan would have supported our efforts to expand stem-cell research.
   a. transfer
   b. glittering generalities
   c. card stacking
   d. bandwagon

_____ 10. It is my privilege to introduce our company president—the go-to guy, the man of decisive action and vision, the man who seeks solutions. Because of his leadership, our corporation has become a world class organization.
   a. transfer
   b. glittering generalities
   c. card stacking
   d. plain folks

Name _____ Section _____ Date _____ Score (number correct) _____ x 10 = _____

A. Directions: Identify the fallacy used in each of the following items.

_____1. Vegetarianism is much better for you because you eliminate all meat from your diet.
     a. false cause
     b. begging the question
     c. either-or
     d. straw man

_____2. Wear Oleander perfume, and love will come into your life.
     a. false comparison
     b. straw man
     c. false cause
     d. either-or

_____3. To win in business, as in war, you need a powerful weapon. Torpedo your competition with AdRite Advertising Firm. Let us give you the weapons with which to win.
     a. straw man
     b. false cause
     c. begging the question
     d. false comparison

_____4. If you are compassionate, humane, and moral, then you are for stem-cell research.
     a. straw man
     b. false cause
     c. false comparison
     d. either-or

_____5. Professor Merley is as stingy with high grades as Scrooge was with money in Dickens' *A Christmas Carol*.
     a. false comparison
     b. straw man
     c. false cause
     d. either-or

B. Directions: Identify the propaganda technique used in each of the following items.

_____6. We, the members of Our Flag Forever, vow our allegiance to the Flag of the United States, which represents our noblest and most precious ideals.
     a. transfer
     b. glittering generalities
     c. name-calling
     d. plain folks

_____7. The SuperCharge XL is the best new car on the market because it is sleek, fast, and irresistibly beautiful.
     a. transfer
     b. testimonial
     c. bandwagon
     d. glittering generalities

_____8. Olympic champion Michael Phelps endorses Nike swim wear.
     a. testimonial
     b. transfer
     c. glittering generalities
     d. bandwagon

_____9. A commercial features a series of before and after pictures of several men and women who have lost more than 30 pounds using Dr. B's Body Beautiful exercise and diet plan. As the pictures of each person are shown, each individual describes his or her success with the program.
     a. testimonial
     b. transfer
     c. glittering generalities
     d. bandwagon

C. Directions: Read the following fictitious advertisement. Identify the detail that was **omitted** from the advertisement for the purpose of card stacking.

_____10. RapiDiet is a medically safe weight-loss program that can produce an effective weight loss of up to one and one-half pounds a day by adjusting a person's metabolism. With RapiDiet, you will achieve safe and rapid weight loss with little discomfort. RapiDiet uses an amino acid tablet supplement known as Growth Hormone Releaser (GHR), a potassium supplement, a daily multi-vitamin, and a 1200–1300-calorie daily diet. Taken before bedtime, GHR burns fat by triggering growth hormones, which then quickens your metabolic rate. In addition, the RapiDiet program uses Synthroid, a thyroid hormone, which also accelerates your metabolic rate. Lose weight safely and rapidly with RapiDiet.

     a. RapiDiet provides protein supplements through powdered puddings and drinks.
     b. RapiDiet contains GHR, which burns fat and quickens your metabolic rate.
     c. The Food and Drug Administration has not approved the drug Synthroid to be safe and effective for the treatment of obesity or weight control.
     d. Most people who use RapiDiet experience noticeable weight loss within several weeks.

CHAPTER 13: ADVANCED ARGUMENTS: PERSUASIVE TECHNIQUES
Lab 13.6 MASTERY TEST 2

Name _____ Section _____ Date _____ Score (number correct) _____ x 10 = _____

A. Directions: Identify the fallacy used in each of the following items.

____1. If you don't shop with us, you might as well throw your money away. Only here are you guaranteed to save three cents on every dollar. Shop with us, or lose out on the best deal in town.
   a. either-or
   b. straw man
   c. false cause
   d. false comparison

____2. Laws are to society what discipline is in the home. Just as children do not understand all the reasons for each and every rule in the house, citizens do not have to understand all the reasons a good law is needed.
   a. begging the question
   b. false cause
   c. false comparison
   d. straw man

____3. Those who oppose a minimum wage fear the success of others.
   a. personal attack
   b. false comparison
   c. either-or
   d. begging the question

____4. The lack of a minimum wage acts upon our society like a cancerous disease destroying the economic health of millions of families.
   a. begging the question
   b. false cause
   c. either-or
   d. false comparison

____5. Celine Ortega supports stem-cell research just to get the votes of families whose loved ones suffer with disabilities and diseases such as Alzheimers.
   a. false comparison
   b. false cause
   c. personal attack
   d. straw man

B. Directions: Identify the propaganda technique used in each of the following items.

_____6. Dale Earnhardt Jr. drives a car sponsored by Budweiser in the NASCAR races.
    a. bandwagon
    b. transfer
    c. plain folks
    d. glittering generalities

_____7. Buy SureGrip hammers. These hammers are the best, and they were designed with you and all your everyday household needs in mind.
    a. card stacking
    b. name-calling
    c. plain folks
    d. glittering generalities

_____8. We condemn the cowardly and dastardly attack upon the Flag of the United States and the Pledge of Allegiance by Cita Zen, a traitor of all that is decent.
    a. name calling
    b. testimonial
    c. plain folks
    d. glittering generalities

_____9. I do not seek public office out of the need for power; indeed I take up the cross of service with the humility of one who is called to fulfill a holy mission.
    a. transfer
    b. bandwagon
    c. name-calling
    d. plain folks

C. Directions: Read the following fictitious advertisement. Identify the detail that was **omitted** from the advertisement for the purpose of card-stacking.

_____10. Everyone should have a Jack Russell terrier. The Jack Russell is a happy, bold, and energetic dog. These dogs are extremely loyal and intelligent. They dogs make great pets as they harbor all the wonderful traits of man's best friend. You can see for yourself the endearing qualities of the Jack Russell, Eddie, on the popular sitcom *Frasier*. Since this show has been aired, the popularity of Jack Russells has increased remarkably.
    a. Jack Russells are incredibly loving and devoted.
    b. Jack Russells are little dogs that can fit easily into a small apartment.
    c. Jack Russells are relatively smart dogs and easy to train.
    d. Jack Russells need a lot of exercise, which includes a minimum of a one-hour walk and several hours of play each day.

PRACTICE TESTS FOR

FLORIDA COLLEGE BASIC SKILLS EXIT READING TEST

TEXAS HIGHER EDUCATION ASSESSMENT TEST

THE EFFECTIVE READER

AWARENESS INVENTORIES

FLORIDA COLLEGE BASIC SKILLS EXIT TEST

TEXAS HIGHER EDUCATION ASSESSMENT TEST

DIAGNOSTIC TEST FOR *THE EFFECTIVE READER*

SUMMARY SHEET OF SCORES

Name _____ Date _____

Objective: To practice for the *Florida College Basic Skills Exit Reading Test*.

Take the practice test, *Florida College Basic Skills Exit Reading Test*, in your textbook. Fill
in the correct answer for each numbered item. Be sure to choose only one answer for each numbered item.

_____ 1. _____ 15. _____ 28.

_____ 2. _____ 16. _____ 29.

_____ 3. _____ 17. _____ 30.

_____ 4. _____ 18. _____ 31.

_____ 5. _____ 19. _____ 32.

_____ 6. _____ 20. _____ 33.

_____ 7. _____ 21. _____ 34.

_____ 8. _____ 22. _____ 35.

_____ 9. _____ 23. _____ 36.

_____ 10. _____ 24. _____ 37.

_____ 11. _____ 25. _____ 38.

_____ 12. _____ 26. _____ 39.

_____ 13. _____ 27. _____ 40.

_____ 14.

Name _____ Date _____

Objective: To gain more practice for the *Florida College Basic Skills Exit Reading Test*.

Fill in the correct answer for each numbered item. Be sure to choose only one answer for each numbered item.

_____ 1. _____ 15. _____ 28.

_____ 2. _____ 16. _____ 29.

_____ 3. _____ 17. _____ 30.

_____ 4. _____ 18. _____ 31.

_____ 5. _____ 19. _____ 32.

_____ 6. _____ 20. _____ 33.

_____ 7. _____ 21. _____ 34.

_____ 8. _____ 22. _____ 35.

_____ 9. _____ 23. _____ 36.

_____ 10. _____ 24. _____ 37.

_____ 11. _____ 25. _____ 38.

_____ 12. _____ 26. _____ 39.

_____ 13. _____ 27. _____ 40.

_____ 14.

Name _____ Date _____

Objective: To practice for the *Texas Higher Education Assessment Test*.

Take the practice test, *Texas Higher Education Assessment Test*, in your textbook. Fill in the correct answer for each numbered item. Be sure to choose only one answer for each numbered item.

_____ 1. _____ 15. _____ 28.

_____ 2. _____ 16. _____ 29.

_____ 3. _____ 17. _____ 30.

_____ 4. _____ 18. _____ 31.

_____ 5. _____ 19. _____ 32.

_____ 6. _____ 20. _____ 33.

_____ 7. _____ 21. _____ 34.

_____ 8. _____ 22. _____ 35.

_____ 9. _____ 23. _____ 36.

_____ 10. _____ 24. _____ 37.

_____ 11. _____ 25. _____ 38.

_____ 12. _____ 26. _____ 39.

_____ 13. _____ 27. _____ 40.

_____ 14.

Name _____ Date _____

Objective: To gain more practice for the *Texas Higher Education Assessment Test*.

Fill in the correct answer for each numbered item. Be sure to choose only one answer for each numbered item.

_____ 1. _____ 15. _____ 28.

_____ 2. _____ 16. _____ 29.

_____ 3. _____ 17. _____ 30.

_____ 4. _____ 18. _____ 31.

_____ 5. _____ 19. _____ 32.

_____ 6. _____ 20. _____ 33.

_____ 7. _____ 21. _____ 34.

_____ 8. _____ 22. _____ 35.

_____ 9. _____ 23. _____ 36.

_____ 10. _____ 24. _____ 37.

_____ 11. _____ 25. _____ 38.

_____ 12. _____ 26. _____ 39.

_____ 13. _____ 27. _____ 40.

_____ 14.

196

Name _____ Date _____

Objective: To discover strengths and areas for improvement in reading comprehension and critical reading.

Take the practice test for *The Effective Reader*, in your textbook. Fill in the correct answer for each numbered item. Be sure to choose only one answer for each numbered item.

_____ 1. _____ 15. _____ 28.

_____ 2. _____ 16. _____ 29.

_____ 3. _____ 17. _____ 30.

_____ 4. _____ 18. _____ 31.

_____ 5. _____ 19. _____ 32.

_____ 6. _____ 20. _____ 33.

_____ 7. _____ 21. _____ 34.

_____ 8. _____ 22. _____ 35.

_____ 9. _____ 23. _____ 36.

_____ 10. _____ 24. _____ 37.

_____ 11. _____ 25. _____ 38.

_____ 12. _____ 26. _____ 39.

_____ 13. _____ 27. _____ 40.

_____ 14.

197

Name _____ Date _____

Objective: To discover strengths and areas for improvement in reading comprehension and critical reading.

Fill in the correct answer for each numbered item. Be sure to choose only one answer for each numbered item.

_____ 1. _____ 15. _____ 28.

_____ 2. _____ 16. _____ 29.

_____ 3. _____ 17. _____ 30.

_____ 4. _____ 18. _____ 31.

_____ 5. _____ 19. _____ 32.

_____ 6. _____ 20. _____ 33.

_____ 7. _____ 21. _____ 34.

_____ 8. _____ 22. _____ 35.

_____ 9. _____ 23. _____ 36.

_____ 10. _____ 24. _____ 37.

_____ 11. _____ 25. _____ 38.

_____ 12. _____ 26. _____ 39.

_____ 13. _____ 27. _____ 40.

_____ 14.

Name _____ Date _____

Scores: % Correct   % Correct

Passage A   _____   Passage E   _____

Passage B   _____   Passage F   _____

Passage C   _____   Passage G   _____

Passage D   _____

The Reading Section of the *Florida State Basic Skills Exit Test* is based on the skills listed below. Circle the number of questions that you missed. Locate pages in your textbook that will help you develop each specific skill. Write out a study plan.

Passage/Question #	Skill
A4, A5, D6, E4, F4, G3	**Determine the meaning of words and phrases.**
AI, A7, CI, D2, EI, E4, GI, G6, FI, F2	**Understand the main idea and supporting details in written material.**
A2, A3, B2, B3, C2, D3, D5, E2, F3, G2, G5	**Identify a writer's purpose, point of view, and intended meaning.**
A6, DI, E3, F5	**Analyze the relationship among ideas in written material.**
B4, C3, D4, G4	**Use critical reasoning skills to evaluate written material.**
BI, F7	**Apply study skills to reading assignments.**

Plan of Action:

_____

_____

_____

_____

_____

_____

_____

_____

_____

_____

_____

_____

_____

_____

_____

_____

_____

_____

Name _____ Date _____

Scores: % Correct   % Correct

Passage A   _____   Passage E   _____

Passage B   _____   Passage F   _____

Passage C   _____   Passage G   _____

Passage D   _____

The Reading Section of the THEA Test is based on the skills listed below. Circle the number of questions that you missed. Locate pages in your textbook that will help you develop each specific skill. Write out a study plan.

Passage/Question #	Skill
A4, A5, D6, E4, F4, G3	**Determine the meaning of words and phrases.**
AI, A7, CI, D2, EI, E4, GI, G6, FI, F2	**Understand the main idea and supporting details in written material.**
A2, A3, B2, B3, C2, D3, D5, E2, F3, G2, G5	**Identify a writer's purpose, point of view, and intended meaning.**
A6, DI, E3, F5	**Analyze the relationship among ideas in written material.**
B4, C3, D4, G4	**Use critical reasoning skills to evaluate written material.**
BI, F7	**Apply study skills to reading assignments.**

Plan of Action:

_____

_____

_____

_____

_____

_____

_____

_____

_____

_____

_____

_____

_____

_____

_____

_____

_____

Name _____ Date _____

Scores: % Correct   % Correct

Passage A   _____   Passage C   _____

Passage B   _____   Passage D   _____

The Diagnostic Test for *The Effective Reader* is based on the skills listed below. Circle the number of questions that you missed. Locate pages in your textbook that will help you develop each specific skill. Write out a study plan.

Passage/Question #	Skill	Textbook Pages
A6, A7, B7, B8, C1, D5, D6	**Vocabulary**	_____
A1, A8, B2, C2, C4, D1	**Main idea**	_____
C3, C10, D9	**Supporting Details**	_____
A3, A4, B3, C6	**Thought Patterns**	_____
A5, B5, B6, C5, D7	**Transitions**	_____
A2, A9, C8, C9	**Tone and Purpose**	_____
A9, C7, D8	**Fact/Opinion**	_____
A10, B10, D2, D3, D4	**Inferences**	_____

203

Plan of Action:

_____

_____

_____

_____

_____

_____

_____

_____

_____

_____

_____

_____

_____

_____

_____

_____

204

	SCORE
Chapter 1: A Reading System for Effective Readers	
Lab 1.1 Practice Exercise 1	
Lab 1.2 Practice Exercise 2	
Lab 1.3 Review Test 1	
Lab 1.4 Review Test 2	
Lab 1.5 Mastery Test 1	
Lab 1.6 Mastery Test 2	
Chapter 2: Vocabulary and Dictionary Skills	
Lab 2.1 Practice Exercise 1	
Lab 2.2 Practice Exercise 2	
Lab 2.3 Review Test 1	
Lab 2.4 Review Test 2	
Lab 2.5 Mastery Test 1	
Lab 2.6 Mastery Test 2	
Chapter 3: Stated Main Ideas	
Lab 3.1 Practice Exercise 1	
Lab 3.2 Practice Exercise 2	
Lab 3.3 Review Test 1	
Lab 3.4 Review Test 2	
Lab 3.5 Mastery Test 1	
Lab 3.6 Mastery Test 2	
Chapter 4: Implied Main Ideas and Implied Central Ideas	
Lab 4.1 Practice Exercise 1	
Lab 4.2 Practice Exercise 2	
Lab 4.3 Review Test 1	
Lab 4.4 Review Test 2	
Lab 4.5 Mastery Test 1	
Lab 4.6 Mastery Test 2	
Chapter 5: Supporting Details	
Lab 5.1 Practice Exercise 1	
Lab 5.2 Practice Exercise 2	
Lab 5.3 Review Test 1	
Lab 5.4 Review Test 2	
Lab 5.5 Mastery Test 1	
Lab 5.6 Mastery Test 2	
Chapter 6: Outlines and Concept Maps	
Lab 6.1 Practice Exercise 1	
Lab 6.2 Practice Exercise 2	
Lab 6.3 Review Test 1	
Lab 6.4 Review Test 2	
Lab 6.5 Mastery Test 1	
Lab 6.6 Mastery Test 2	

Chapter 7: Transitions and Thought Patterns	
Lab 7.1 Practice Exercise 1	
Lab 7.2 Practice Exercise 2	
Lab 7.3 Review Test 1	
Lab 7.4 Review Test 2	
Lab 7.5 Mastery Test 1	
Lab 7.6 Mastery Test 2	
Chapter 8: More Thought Patterns	
Lab 8.1 Practice Exercise 1	
Lab 8.2 Practice Exercise 2	
Lab 8.3 Review Test 1	
Lab 8.4 Review Test 2	
Lab 8.5 Mastery Test 1	
Lab 8.6 Mastery Test 2	
Chapter 9: Fact and Opinion	
Lab 9.1 Practice Exercise 1	
Lab 9.2 Practice Exercise 2	
Lab 9.3 Review Test 1	
Lab 9.4 Review Test 2	
Lab 9.5 Mastery Test 1	
Lab 9.6 Mastery Test 2	
Chapter 10: Tone and Purpose	
Lab 10.1 Practice Exercise 1	
Lab 10.2 Practice Exercise 2	
Lab 10.3 Review Test 1	
Lab 10.4 Review Test 2	
Lab 10.5 Mastery Test 1	
Lab 10.6 Mastery Test 2	
Chapter 11: Inferences	
Lab 11.1 Practice Exercise 1	
Lab 11.2 Practice Exercise 2	
Lab 11.3 Review Test 1	
Lab 11.4 Review Test 2	
Lab 11.5 Mastery Test 1	
Lab 11.6 Mastery Test 2	
Chapter 12: The Basics of Argument	
Lab 12.1 Practice Exercise 1	
Lab 12.2 Practice Exercise 2	
Lab 12.3 Review Test 1	
Lab 12.4 Review Test 2	
Lab 12.5 Mastery Test 1	
Lab 12.6 Mastery Test 2	
Chapter 13: Advanced Argument: Persuasive Techniques	
Lab 13.1 Practice Exercise 1	
Lab 13.2 Practice Exercise 2	
Lab 13.3 Review Test 1	
Lab 13.4 Review Test 2	
Lab 13.5 Mastery Test 1	
Lab 13.6 Mastery Test 2	

Practice Tests	
Practice Tests for the *Florida College Basic Skills Exit Reading Test*	
Practice Tests for the *Texas Higher Education Assessment Test*	
Practice Tests for *The Effective Reader*	
Skills Awareness Inventory: Florida Basic Exit Test	
Skills Awareness Inventory: THEA	
Skills Awareness Inventory: *The Effective Reader*	